# Basic Cake Decorating
## Techniques, Ideas and Projects

SHELLY BAKER

A Quintet book
First published in the UK in 2014 by
Search Press Ltd
Wellwood
North Farm Road
Tunbridge Wells
Kent TN2 3DR
www.searchpress.com

ISBN: 978-1-78221-041-2
QTT.ICIE

This book was conceived, designed and produced by:
Quintet Publishing
4th Floor, Sheridan House
114-116 Western Road
Hove, East Sussex BN3 1DD

Project Editor: Emma Callery
Designer: Rod Teasdale
Photographer: Simon Pask
Food Stylist: Robert Watson
Art Director: Michael Charles
Managing Editor: Emma Bastow
Publisher: Mark Searle

10 9 8 7 6 5 4 3 2 1

Printed in China by Toppan Leefung PTE. LTD.

# Contents

# Introduction

Cakes are milestone markers for most occasions. I can barely remember an event when I was growing up that my Mum didn't make a perfectly crafted cake for. It became a family tradition of giving her bigger and more challenging ideas to attempt with each new cake. Each time she would rise to the occasion and produce something that left us all in awe of her.

Sadly, my Mum passed away before I could learn from her, but as she left me with a young brother, I decided I would take on the role of the family cake decorator. It was a steep learning curve, but I taught myself a little each day. I found I had a real flare for cake decorating and it soon became a great passion of mine. Seeing my brother's face when I presented him with his ninth birthday cake was worth all of the hours it had taken. It was a giant cupcake decorated in the colours of his favourite football team. That day I decided I wanted to turn these skills into a business.

Within four years I have gone from producing themed cakes and cupcakes to order, to teaching classes on cake decorating. One of my proudest moments was winning my two cake awards at an international show. It means so much to be appreciated by those who know more than I could ever begin to learn.

Giving cake decorating classes is what I enjoy the most as I love passing on these skills to others. Knowing that the precious memories of birthday cakes will go on for years to come and for many different families makes the classes even more enjoyable.

This book takes you step by step through both basic and advanced cake decorating skills and ideas. All of the cakes have been designed to build on the skills described, so that even the most complex cakes seem manageable.

Each of the cakes and cupcakes are not only simple to make, but they also use minimum equipment. With just a few tools and your imagination you can produce amazing results. From piping skills to sculpting cakes and working with different modelling mediums, there is an abundance of skills here for you to learn.

My aim for this book is for it to become an indispensable addition to your kitchen and something that helps you carry on the tradition of baking for your family and friends year after year.

SHELLY BAKER

# Materials and equipment

It's easy to get excited about starting to decorate cakes and to rush into purchasing every tool you can see in the shop, but beware ending up with tools sitting in your tool kit that are never needed. Instead, use this chapter to learn about the essential tools, many of which are used over and over again. While there are some pieces of equipment that you make do with before you buy the exact tools – for example, using a regular dinner knife instead of a palette knife – there are others that you really cannot afford to do without, such as piping tips and icing smoothers.

# General equipment

When purchasing cake decorating tools and equipment, remember they are not only available in your local cake supply shops, but online too. Do not forget to check out local small independent shops as many are very competitively priced. It's always best to shop around before you make your final purchase.

### Cake boards

You can purchase cake boards in many different shapes and sizes. They are most often 2 cm (3/4 in.) deep and made from a sturdy material to support the weight of the cake. It is important to always choose a cake board that is 5–10 cm (2–4 in.) bigger than your cake, not only to protect the cake from damage during transport or display, but also to add to the overall design.

### Cake card

The bottom tier of a cake is first placed on a thin cake card that, like cake boards, is available in many different shapes and sizes. Make sure you always use one that is the same size as the cake.

### Cake tins

There are so many different cake tins available to purchase now that you may find it overwhelming. The main thing to think about is what size cakes you will make the most. If you are baking for a family, you will probably not use anything bigger than an 20 cm (8 in.) round cake tin. In fact, for the majority of the recipes in this book I use a 18 cm (7 in.) round cake tin. An ideal tin for baking cupcakes would be a 12-hole muffin tin.

Some of the recipes do make use of other tin sizes, so before making any of them, check that you have the appropriate size first. Shaped tins are available from many retailers. I would recommend a giant cupcake tin, as you can use it not only to make giant cupcakes but also it has a great base shape for carving out other designs.

Use stainless steel tins; they are easy to clean and evenly distribute the heat. Do not worry about buying non-stick tins – cake release spray works on stainless steel.

### Cake wire

A cake cutting wire is available from all cake supply shops. It slides easily through a cake horizontally, enabling you to level the surface.

### Cake release spray

The traditional method of greasing and flouring your tin can leave a powdered surface on your cake that is hard to remove. Cake release spray is a fantastic alternative. It is easy to apply and, used sparingly, will help you remove your cakes from the tin easily.

### Craft knife

While any sharp knife will be good to start with, a craft knife is an important part of your cake decorating kit. From trimming the excess off of a cake, to cutting straight lines with a ruler, it has a wide range of uses.

### Embossing folders

These are plastic folders with a positive and negative pattern on them. They are primarily used in card making but they work wonders on fondant, giving a great embossed effect. They are available in most craft shops in the paper department, but I am sure that more of them will soon appear in the cake decorating aisles too. Remember that if you are using these with fondant, do not use them with paper too as it will not be following food safety guidelines.

### Extruder gun

The Sugarcraft extruder gun is a fantastic tool that you can use for endless effects, such as making hair and ropes as well as singular lengths of fondant that are ideal for edging a cake where it joins to the board. An extruder gun comes with sixteen different discs to insert into the end and use as nozzles. They range from a tiny single hole to multiple openings and even a basket weave shape.

The gun is easy to use with warm fondant. As the fondant firms up, it becomes harder to push through the tip of the gun. The fondant must be warm to be pliable.

### Palette knife

From straight to angled, you can purchase these in many different styles. When working with smaller cakes, a short, straight palette knife is ideal, but when working with larger cakes, a larger angled palette knife helps you cover both the top and side surfaces of the cake. The palette knife will be a staple item in your cake tool kit. It is ideal for spreading fillings and coating cakes.

### Icing smoothers

When you are making square or round cakes, you will need to use icing smoothers to help you achieve a perfectly flat surface. They are white plastic paddles with a smooth surface that glides against fondant effortlessly. Use them with a back and forth motion all around the surface of the cake. It will help you remove any air bubbles and adhere fondant to the cake.

### Icing spacers

It is hard to get your fondant rolled out to the same thickness without using icing spacers. The two metal or plastic strips allow you to position your rolling pin at the correct height and angle, to create a perfectly even surface.

### Jumbo straws

When you are making stacked cakes, you can use dowels to hold up the layers. If you are only stacking small cakes, then you can use jumbo drinking straws. They are food safe and easier to cut than traditional dowels.

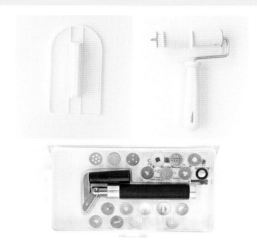

### Level

A small lightweight spirit level is a handy tool to have in your kit. These can be purchased easily from any DIY shop. You must ensure this is only used for cake decorating to avoid cross-contamination.

### Lollipop sticks

These paper sticks are ideal for making letters and numbers stand up or to hold cake pops. They are most often white but since cake pops became so popular, they are now available in a wide array of colours.

### Marble cutting board

This is an essential tool when working with chocolate. When making decorations with chocolate, you will need a cold surface. Marble stays cool for much longer than any other surface.

### Metal scraper

Used for achieving a neat finish on the side of a cake, this tool is really essential if you are looking for a perfectly smooth frosting or ganache.

### Moulds

From tiny details to larger display decorations, you can get moulds in so many different shapes and sizes. These are mainly made out of silicone. They are flexible and their non-stick surface makes them an ideal thing to put gum paste into.

### Multi-ribbon cutter

When you need to cut identical size strips of fondant, there is no better tool than the multi-ribbon cutter. It allows you to cut thicknesses between 3 mm and 50 mm (1/8 in. and 2 in.). A selection of cutting wheels enables you to cut both straight edges or wavy ones, or even a combination of both to give the design a whole new look.

### Non-slip matting

Place a non-slip mat between two surfaces that would otherwise be unstable and slippery. A non-slip mat can be used for things other than cake decorating. Many homeware shops sell low-cost alternatives.

### Paintbrushes

From ultra-fine brushes for painting facial details, to large rounded tipped brushes for blending powder onto a cake, there are brushes for all your needs. I prefer to work with synthetic bristles, as I find they keep their shape better and it is easier to be more precise with painting or blending. Wash your brushes well in warm water and always stand them in a beaker to dry or the bristles will spread and your brush will be ruined.

### Paint palette

Any plastic paint palette is handy when you are decorating cakes. It enables you to mix your own paints, food colouring pastes, powders and lustre dusts with clear alcohol or dipping solution. A white plate is a good substitute if you don't have a palette on hand. A paint palette also serves as a great fondant flower drying tray. The small sections hold the flower shapes perfectly and you can dry several of them at a time.

### Ribbons and lace

There are so many different sizes, colours and types of ribbon that I won't try to list them all here. Ribbon is a staple item to have on hand because it is just the right thickness to edge your cake board with. Simply run a glue stick along the back of the ribbon and attach it to the edge of the board to finish any cake perfectly.

### Rolling pin

This tool doesn't need much of an explanation, but do your research before you buy a rolling pin. You will need a small one for making cupcakes and decorations, and a large one for rolling out cake covering. They are available in wood, vinyl, metal and even silicone coated. I would suggest buying a vinyl rolling pin as they have a smooth surface and come in many sizes.

### Ruler

A ruler is essential for helping you achieve straight lines.

### Scissors

A sharp pair of scissors will be really useful to have on hand when decorating cakes. Keep a separate pair for cake decorating so you do not have to worry about food contamination.

### Texture comb

Texture combs are available in many different patterns and are usually made from a hard plastic material. These are perfect for creating stunning last-minute cakes with very little effort.

### Cocktail sticks

These small wooden sticks are great for applying small amounts of food colouring to things. They have many uses and are considered a valuable piece of your cake decorating kit.

### Turntable

While you don't necessarily need to buy a professional turntable, having the ability to spin your cake easily while working is vital. Turntables are available with or without non-slip matting.

### Uncooked spaghetti

I know you are thinking, spaghetti...in a cake? I have never used it that way before. The spaghetti is actually for helping with the structure of models. It's an edible medium and although it wouldn't be tasty if eaten, you will be safe in the knowledge that if you use this instead of cocktail sticks that you aren't risking the safety of the person eating the model.

---

#### TIP

**Vinyl rolling pins can produce static electricity, so use kitchen roll to wipe across the surface of the pin before starting to work. This will help you remove any fibres that have collected on the rolling pin.**

---

# Piping tools

The same piping tools are used for piping with frosting or royal icing and are invaluable for creating attractive cakes, so it's worth investing in a basic kit.

### Piping bags

There are several types of piping bags you can use. I like to use the disposable piping bags because you can cut the end and fit it with any tip. A reusable bag is ideal if you do a lot of piping. Use a coupler at the end so you can change the tips easily.

### Piping tips

Also known as piping nozzles, piping tips are available in many shapes, sizes and styles. I like to use a small selection of piping tips to create many different patterns and effects. The tips listed below make the ideal starter kit, as they cover the frequently used techniques. However, as your skills develop, you will quickly find other ways to use them.

---

## PIPING TIPS:
## A STARTER KIT

Piping tips are produced by many different companies. Although they may use the same numbers, I have found that this does not mean that they are the same piping tip. So to get the best results, use the make and number given with each skill and recipe.

### WILTON

No. 1A round decorating tip
No. 1M open star decorating tip
No. 2D drop flower decorating tip
No. 1 round decorating tip
No. 7 round decorating tip
No. 104 petal decorating tip
No. 127 petal decorating tip
No. 233 multi-opening decorating tip

### PME

FT070 frill tip

---

### TIPS

- The quality of piping tips varies enormously. The main thing to remember when purchasing a tip is how often you will be using it. If you have a tip that you use daily, then you will ideally want to purchase a metal version of it because the plastic tips are less robust, and not made to withstand daily use.

- Wash your piping tips by hand as you will tarnish the metal in the dishwasher.

# Hand tools

You will find these tools invaluable and they each have their own uses. When choosing which hand tools to buy, I recommend the PME branded set, as it holds every type of tool you will need and they are very good quality. While there are many hand tools available, the four tools listed here are those I find most useful and will equip you to make the projects in the book.

### Ball tool

This tool has a different sized ball at each end. The small ball is ideal for adding dimples to models, making ears and even nostrils. The bigger ball is mainly used for thinning the edges of petals and making ruffles. The large rounded surface means it can thin fondant and gum paste without tearing it.

### Cone tool

Ideal for using with fondant, this tool enables you to make holes in the fondant easily. Each end of the tool has a different sized cone so you have the option of a small indentation or a large one.

### Stitching tool

Just like a pizza wheel, this tool spins at one end and leaves a stitched effect when you roll it across the fondant. Use this tool to add stitches to garments on models or run the tool in a grid pattern to create a quilted effect.

### Scriber tool

This is one of the most versatile tools. The pointed tip is great for sculpting models, hair, smiles and fine details. The smooth rounded tip is ideal for smoothing the surface of fondant, making eye sockets and ridges in the fondant where needed.

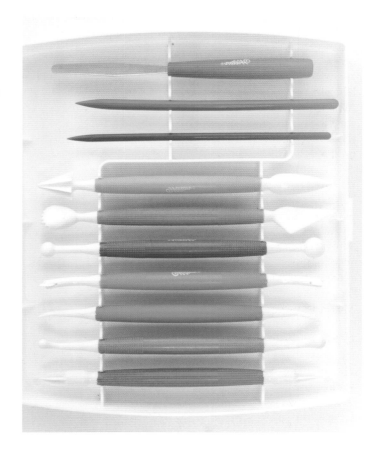

# Cutters

There are many different types of cutters that you can use with both fondant and gum paste. Each are suited to creating particular shapes. Build up your collection slowly according to your chosen cakes and designs.

### Metal cutters

For a neat edge and a precise cut, metal cutters are hard to beat. Often matched with moulds (see pages 9 and 208) to add detail, these cutters are very popular. Metal cutters are also ideal for using to make three-dimensional lettering, cutting through thicker gum paste. Pastry cutters are generally made from metal too, and are often larger in size and less detailed.

### Plastic cutters

Available in many shapes and sizes, plastic cutters can vary widely. When using them, you will need to remove the shape manually using your fingertip or a ball tool. Be gentle so you do not indent the surface of your shape.

### Plunger cutters

These cutters are great because they take the hassle out of releasing the shapes from the cutter itself. Most of the plunger cutters have an embossing element to them (see pages 8 and 158), which helps you add detail and definition to the shape you are creating. For example, a leaf cutter will cut the shape and add the vein detail to the leaf too. Once dried in a cel former (see page 14), you will find the leaf becomes more lifelike.

### Texture cutter sets

Texture cutters are great as they not only give you a distinct shape, but they also emboss the shape so you have a dual effect. The set used on the Eastern Promise Cake (see page 174) is an ideal starter set, although you can also achieve the same effect for other shapes by embossing the fondant and then using cutters to achieve the shapes.

# Three-dimensional shapes

When you are making flowers and other three-dimensional shapes to adorn your beautiful cakes, you will want them to look as lifelike and fabulous as possible. I will tell you about the essential tools to achieve perfect decorations.

### CMC powder

When you are making cake decorations you will want them to hold their shape, but you won't be able to do this simply using fondant. You will find it goes limp over time and your hard work will be ruined. However, all you have to do is add some CMC powder (the shortened name for carboxymethyl cellulose) to the fondant and it will hold its shape and become firm. This is how you produce a gum paste and it is ideal for modelling figures and structures too (see pages 36 and 204–249).

### Cel formers and drying foam

Dry your shapes in cel formers or drying foam. These provide a surface to help them keep their three-dimensional shape.

When buying drying foam for flowers, make sure you buy the raw type that has not been sprayed with a fire retardant chemical. The same foam is used for sound proofing studios and this chemical will make your flowers inedible.

Cel formers are made from plastic. In humid climates you will find these are not as good for drying your flowers since the surface will not let the paste breathe and dry. If you have this problem, you can add a little corn flour to the cel former so it does not stick.

### Foam drying balls

This ingenious idea was first designed by Purple Cupcakes in the UK. They ship these worldwide and I must say they are a great help. When you want to create domed top cupcakes, these foam balls allow you to place a circle of fondant over them to dry. Once dry, you can transfer the fondant to the cupcake and, voila!, you have the perfect dome. They are available in packs of six, so you will either need to work in small batches at a time or buy two packs of the foam balls.

### Styrofoam

When you are making cake pops or stemmed flowers you will need to dry them standing up. Styrofoam is a great way to achieve this. The dense foam allows you to poke the stems or sticks into the foam, which holds them in place while they dry.

# Food colourings

When you are making cakes and decorating them you will definitely want to add some colouring to either your sponge or the frosting. There are many ways you can do this. Here is a list of the most popular products.

### Food colouring paste

This is a concentrated, thick paste for colouring food and frosting. You can use this to colour your sponge cake at the preparation stage or your fondant before you roll it out. Add a small amount at a time so that you can build the colour tone of your choice (see page 38).

Synthetic colours are vibrant and bold, so you can achieve a wide spectrum of colour. They are robust and withstand daylight well, but colour from a synthetic colourant will deepen slightly overnight. It is better to colour your fondant the day before you need to use it.

### Natural food colouring paste

Natural food colourings are widely available through your local cake supply shop. Brands such as PME, have seen that there is a need for these natural colourings for cakes and sweet treats. Although synthetic food colouring provides a wider range of colours, you can easily blend two natural colourings together to make any colour you want.

Natural food colourings fade very easily in daylight so keep the cake covered until you are ready to present it. Though the colours are not as vibrant and are more muted than the synthetic ones, they are easier to digest for young children and those with food allergies.

Natural food colouring tends to have a shorter shelf life, so only buy the colours you will use most often at first.

### Food colouring powder

Often labelled as petal dust or powder, similar to the lustre dusts but without any shimmer. The colours are deep and can also be used either dry, or mixed with clear alcohol or dipping solution (see page 16) to make a paint.

These powdered colourings are great for adding some colour to faces made from fondant or depth to flowers. Many of the recipes in this book show you how to use them in different ways.

As a slightly different option, you can purchase Sugarflair, an extra concentrated food colour. Available in white, red and black, these powdered colours help you to increase the intensity of your other food colourings.

### Lustre dust

You may have seen many cakes adorned with pretty shimmering flowers and decorations. These are made using lustre dusts. The powder can be used dry with a small or large paintbrush, depending on the project. To use it, gently dust the lustre over the decoration and build it up to the desired effect.

An alternative to using the lustre dust dry is to make it into a paint. Add clear alcohol or dipping solution (see page 16), one drop at a time and mix with a brush until you achieve the desired consistency. You can then paint straight onto fondant.

### Lustre spray

If you are looking to make a large cake sparkle and shimmer, these sprays are ideal. The aerosol cans are filled with lustre dust and a clear alcohol that evaporates in seconds. You will need to spray it in a ventilated room and cover any part of the cake or area surrounding it that you don't want the spray to reach.

You can also purchase spray glaze in a can, which adds a clear film to the cake or decoration. The glaze gives the surface of the cake a glossy appearance and heightens the colour. This is ideal for things such as marzipan fruits, where you need a realistic sheen on the surface.

### Edible food pens

If you don't feel comfortable painting on a cake, edible food pens are a great alternative. Much like a normal felt tipped pen they have a pointed nib and when used on dry fondant or gum paste you will find them easy to write with.

# Ingredients

Most icing and frosting projects only really require a few key ingredients, but those ingredients must be used for their intended purposes to make your finished cakes a success. The main ingredients you will need to practise the skills in this book and create the cake projects at the end of each chapter are listed here.

### Candy melts

These candy drops can be melted to pour into moulds or to cover cakes. They are also ideal for covering cake pops as their bright colours are really appealing. Outside of the United States, these are usually only availble online.

### Chocolate transfer sheets

These sheets of acetate have been printed with a special ink made from cocoa butter. They are available in many different designs and can be added to chocolate to form fantastic displays (see page 142).

### Clear alcohol or dipping solution

When you are making paint with food colouring powders, pastes and lustre dusts, you need to use clear alcohol, such as vodka, or dipping solution, which is a clear liquid containing alcohol made especially for cake decorating. The alcohol evaporates almost immediately, leaving just the colour in place.

**TIP**

To remove any icing sugar or corn flour marks on a cake, brush on a small amount of clear alcohol.

### Edible glaze

This product is useful for adding a sheen to marzipan models. It is available either in a small pot and is applied with a brush, or in an aerosol can for spraying over the model (for more information, see page 253). Although edible glaze is a great ingredient, it does not usually have a long shelf life, so purchase it as needed because it does not store well once opened. It can be used on any edible item and is often used by pastry chefs to glaze desserts.

### Edible glue

Whether you purchase glue or you make your own (see page 41), edible glue is something you need to have when decorating cakes. You only need a small amount to be effective and it is surprisingly strong too. Many people use a cocktail stick to add glue to something on a cake, but I prefer to use a brush as it allows you to be more precise.

### Fondant

Soft, smooth and silky, this is a cake-covering medium used widely across the world. Sweet in taste, it combines well with cakes of all sizes. You can buy it ready-made or make your own (see pages 34, 38 and 154–203).

### Gum paste

This edible medium dries firm and holds its shape. It is often used for making flowers and figures, and you can roll it incredibly thin or form it into shapes that make a model. Models made from gum paste store well for at least six months, so you can make a few at a time and use them on different cakes. It is a very versatile medium that I use frequently (see pages 36, 38 and 204–249).

### Marzipan

Marzipan is made from ground almonds and can be used as a substitute for fondant. Its unique flavour combines well with some cakes (see pages 37–38 and 250–271).

### Modelling chocolate

Modelling chocolate is a thick medium used to cover a cake. It is similar to gum paste in thickness. It can also be used to model roses and other shapes because it dries firm (see pages 30 and 126–153).

### Printed icing sheet

These are sheets of flat icing printed with a pattern or image. You can either purchase them already printed or you can visit a cake decorating shop to get one done with a pattern of your choice. It is best to use metal cutters with the sheets as plastic cutters don't give a sharp edge to the shape you cut out.

### Sanding sugar

Coloured sugar, known as sanding sugar, is often used to add detail to cupcakes and cake pops. The sugar shimmers when the light hits it – a nice finishing touch to your cake.

# Recipes

Before you get started with icing and frosting, it is important to perfect some basic recipes – there's no point spending hours on gum paste flowers for a dry, tasteless cake. These cake recipes have been specially designed to complement the wide range of icing and frosting skills covered in this book. This chapter also includes cake pops, modelling chocolate, ganache, fondant, marzipan and gum paste – refer back to their simple tutorials as and when you need them.

# Basic sponge cake

This basic sponge cake is very easy to make – simply combine all of the ingredients in a mixer. This cake is also simple to adapt for different occasions. Try adding a flavouring – chocolate, lemon or orange all make delicious sponge cakes.

**MAKES**

Two-layer 18 cm (8 in.) round cake or 12 cupcakes (for other sizes of cake, see the table on page 22)

## EQUIPMENT

*2 x 20 cm (8 in.) round cake tins*

## INGREDIENTS

*200 g (7 oz.) self-raising flour*

*200 g (7 oz.) unsalted butter, softened*

*200 g (7 oz.) caster sugar*

*4 large eggs*

*2 tbsp. vegetable oil*

*2 tsp. vanilla extract*

## FLAVOURINGS (OPTIONAL)

*Chocolate: replace 50 g (2 oz.) of the self-raising flour with cocoa powder and add 50 g (2 oz.) melted Belgian chocolate*

*Lemon: replace the vanilla extract with finely grated zest of 2 lemons*

*Orange: replace the vanilla extract with finely grated zest of 2 oranges*

### STEP 1

Preheat the oven to 160°C (325°F/Gas Mark 3). Spray the cake tins with cake release spray. If you prefer, you can use the traditional method of greasing and flouring your tin (see page 44).

### STEP 2

Put all the ingredients into an electric stand mixer and insert the beater blade. Turn it on and mix the ingredients for about 1 minute on a medium speed, then turn off the mixer and use a spatula to scrape down the bowl and blade, removing any flour residue. Turn the mixer back on again for another minute or until the mixture is very thick. Alternatively, beat the mixture in a large mixing bowl with an electric hand whisk.

### STEP 3

Spoon the batter into the prepared tins and level the mixture with a spatula. Place the cakes in the oven and do not open the oven during the first half of baking because they will start sinking.

### STEP 4

Check the cakes after 30 minutes. If they stick to the sides of the tin, they are not done. Cook for another 5–10 minutes. You will know when the cakes are done by touching one of them in the middle. If it shrinks back and has shrunk down from the sides, it is done (see page 46). Another way to check them is by inserting a thin knife or cocktail stick into the centre. If it comes out clean, the cakes are done.

### STEP 5

Leave cakes to cool in the tins for 10 minutes. Remove the cakes from the tins and place onto a cooling rack to cool completely before decorating.

> #### FURTHERING YOUR SKILLS
>
> - When planning a cake I always use a 24-hour rule, which means that I bake the cake 24 hours before it is needed and allow it to cool completely before attempting to decorate it. It is important to give yourself enough time to decorate a cake, so plan your time wisely so that you're not in a rush.

Use this table to adapt the basic sponge cake recipe on page 20 for your chosen cake tin size.

## ROUND CAKES

| Cake diameter | 10 cm (4 in.) | 13 cm (5 in.) | 15 cm (6 in.) | 18 cm (7 in.) | 20 cm (8 in.) | 23 cm (9 in.) |
|---|---|---|---|---|---|---|
| Self-raising flour | 125 g (4 ½ oz.) | 175 g (6 oz.) | 250 g (9 oz.) | 325 g 12 ½ oz. | 500 g (1 lb. 2 oz.) | 675 g (1 ½ lbs.) |
| Unsalted butter | 75 g (3 oz.) | 115 g (4 oz.) | 175 g (6 oz.) | 225 g (8 oz.) | 350 g (12 oz.) | 450 g (1 lb.) |
| Caster sugar | 75 g (3 oz.) | 115 g (4 oz.) | 175 g (6 oz.) | 225 g (8 oz.) | 350 g (12 oz.) | 450 g (1 lb.) |
| Eggs | 1 ½ | 2 | 3 | 4 | 6 | 8 |
| Vegetable oil | ¾ tbsp. | 1 tbsp. | 1 ⅔ tbsp. | 1 ¾ tbsp. | 2 tbsp. | 2 ¼ tbsp. |
| Vanilla extract | ¾ tsp. | 1 tsp. | 1 ⅔ tsp. | 1 ¾ tsp. | 2 tsp. | 2 ¼ tsp. |

## SQUARE CAKES

| Cake diameter | 8 cm (3 in.) | 10 cm (4 in.) | 13 cm (5 in.) | 15 cm (6 in.) | 18 cm (7 in.) | 20 cm (8 in.) | 23 cm (9 in.) |
|---|---|---|---|---|---|---|---|
| Self-raising flour | 125 g (4 ½ oz.) | 175 g (6 oz.) | 250 g (9 oz.) | 325 g 12 ½ oz. | 500 g (1 lb. 2 oz.) | 675 g (1 ½ lbs.) | 750 g (1 lb. 11 oz.) |
| Unsalted butter | 75 g (3 oz.) | 115 g (4 oz.) | 175 g (6 oz.) | 225 g (8 oz.) | 350 g (12 oz.) | 450 g (1 lb.) | 500 g (1 lb. 2 oz.) |
| Caster sugar | 75 g (3 oz.) | 115 g (4 oz.) | 175 g (6 oz.) | 225 g (8 oz.) | 350 g (12 oz.) | 450 g (1 lb.) | 500 g (1 lb. 2 oz.) |
| Eggs | 1 ½ | 2 | 3 | 4 | 6 | 8 | 9 |
| Vegetable oil | ¾ tbsp. | 1 tbsp. | 1 ⅔ tbsp. | 1 ¾ tbsp. | 2 tbsp. | 2 ¼ tbsp. | 2 ½ tbsp. |
| Vanilla extract | ¾ tsp. | 1 tsp. | 1 ⅔ tsp. | 1 ¾ tsp. | 2 tsp. | 2 ¼ tsp. | 2 ½ tsp. |

# Cupcakes

## EQUIPMENT

*12-hole muffin tin*

*12 cupcake cases*

## MAKES

**12 cupcakes**

### STEP 1

Preheat the oven to 160°C (325°F/Gas Mark 3). Line the muffin tin with the cupcake cases.

### STEP 2

Prepare the cake mix as described in Step 2, page 21.

### STEP 3

Use an ice cream scoop to measure the batter equally into each cupcake case, about $^2/_3$ full, and bake for approximately 20 minutes – do not open the oven during the first 10 minutes. You will know when the cupcakes are done if you touch them and they spring back in the centre.

Another way to check them is by inserting a thin knife or cocktail stick into the centre, if it comes out clean, the cupcakes are done.

### STEP 4

Remove the cupcakes from the tins and place onto a cooling rack. Allow them to cool completely before decorating.

### FURTHERING YOUR SKILLS

- When baking cupcakes, if you find they look like volcanoes, try turning down the temperature of your oven and increasing the baking time slightly. This will help you achieve a more even bake.

- If your cupcake cases start to peel off the cakes, it is often due to a build-up of condensation between the cake and the muffin tin. To avoid this, remove the cupcakes from the tin as soon as they are removed from the oven.

# Madeira cake

When you need a dense cake for carving, Madeira is your best choice. Unlike regular sponge cake, it holds its shape well and is less likely to crumble when being carved. Madeira is most often used without a filling, for carved cakes, as it is less liable to lose its shape that way. However, for regular round and square cakes, you may choose to slice the cake in half horizontally and then use a filling in the same manner as you would a regular sponge cake (see pages 50–53). The flavourings are optional, but they do make the cake extra tasty.

**MAKES**
18 cm (7 in.) round x 7.5 cm (3 in.) deep cake

**EQUIPMENT**

18 cm (7 in.) diameter x 7.5 cm (3 in.) deep cake tin

**INGREDIENTS**

300 g (10 oz.) unsalted butter, softened

300 g (10 oz.) caster sugar

5 large eggs

4 tbsp. milk

1 tsp. vanilla extract

400 g (13 oz.) self-raising flour

**FLAVOURINGS (OPTIONAL)**

Chocolate: replace 75 g (3 oz.) of the self-raising flour with cocoa powder

Lemon: add grated zest of 1 ½ lemons

Orange: add 4 tbsp. orange juice

## STEP 1

Preheat the oven to 160°C (325°F/Gas Mark 3). Spray the cake tin with cake release spray. If you prefer, you may use the traditional method of greasing and then flouring your tin.

## STEP 2

Using an electric hand whisk, cream the butter and sugar together in a bowl until light and fluffy. Lightly beat the eggs with the milk and vanilla extract in a separate bowl. Gradually beat the eggs and milk into the creamed mixture, alternating with the flour.

## STEP 3

Turn the mixture out into the prepared tin and level the mixture with a spatula. Bake in the oven for about 70 minutes or until a knife comes out clean after inserting it into the centre of the cake.

## STEP 4

Remove the cake from the oven and let it cool for 5 minutes before turning out onto a cooling rack. Allow your cake several hours to cool fully before decorating or carving.

### FURTHERING YOUR SKILLS

- Madeira cake keeps for up to two weeks wrapped in wax paper, then cling film, and stored in an airtight container.

- You can make a chocolate Madeira cake by adding cocoa powder to the flour. By adding more or less cocoa powder, you can control how chocolaty you like it. On a cake of this size, it is important not to go over 110 g (4 oz.).

# Cake pops

Cake pops are lots of fun to make AND eat, and they are perfect bite-sized portions for children. The lollipop style of cake pops means they are easy to eat on the go, and they are a popular choice for party favours. This is the basic recipe – see Chocolate Drizzle Cake Pops and Rose Cake Pops on pages 144 and 146 for how to frost them.

**MAKES**
12 plain cake pops

**EQUIPMENT**

*12 cake pop sticks*

*Styrofoam*

**INGREDIENTS**

*12 cupcakes from the basic recipe (see page 23)*

*2–4 tbsp. frosting (see page 28)*

*Small amount of dark chocolate*

### STEP 1

Crumble the cupcakes into the bowl of an electric stand mixer until they are fine crumbs.

### STEP 2

Add the frosting to the bowl and mix thoroughly at a slow speed and then a medium speed until the crumbs and frosting are combined. You will know if the consistency is right when you can squeeze the mixture and it will hold its shape when you let go.

### STEP 3

Divide the mixture into balls about the size of ping-pong balls. Roll them until smooth and place them on a baking tray and then put them in the fridge for at least 30 minutes.

### STEP 4

Melt the chocolate as described on page 129. Then dip the tip of a cake pop stick into the chocolate and press it halfway into a cake ball.

### STEP 5

Stand the cake pop in the styrofoam and repeat with the rest of the cake balls and sticks. Set aside at room temperature for about 2 hours to set fully before decorating.

### CAKE POP QUANTITIES

The best thing about cake pops is that they are a great way to use up cake pieces. While this recipe is for 12 cake pops made from the basic recipe on page 23, if you have small amounts of cake available, bear in mind that one cupcake equals about one cake pop. Add a teaspoon of frosting at a time until the crumbs are just combined.

# Frosting

Frosting is basically a 2:1 ratio of icing sugar to butter, enriched with the flavour of your choice. This type of frosting is ideal for both piping and spreading. It starts out soft and pipes really well. It will also form a slight crust and hold its shape once dry. See pages 72–125 for skills and recipes that feature frosting.

**MAKES**

750 g (1 lb. 11 oz.) frosting (enough to crumb coat a 18 cm (7 in.) round basic sponge cake or 12 cupcakes)

**STEP 1**

Put the butter into the bowl of an electric stand mixer and soften it slightly at a low speed, if necessary.

**STEP 2**

Add the icing sugar, a little at a time, and beat on a medium speed for 1–2 minutes until the mixture is a smooth paste. Beat in flavouring, test the frosting and add more flavouring if necessary.

## INGREDIENTS

*250 g (8 oz.) butter, softened*

*500 g (1 lb. 2 oz.) icing sugar*

## FLAVOURINGS

*2 tsp. vanilla extract*

*50 g (2 oz.) milk, dark or white chocolate, melted (see page 129)*

*Grated zest of 3 lemons or oranges*

*1 tsp. orange blossom extract and 1 tsp. vanilla extract*

*4 tsp. strawberry purée*

*4 tsp. raspberry purée*

# Colouring frosting

You can colour frosting naturally or with synthetic colourings. Flavourings such as fresh strawberry purée give the frosting a pink colouring, and lemon curd turns the frosting a yellow colour. You can also purchase 100 per cent natural colourings.

### STEP 1

Use a cocktail stick to add the colour to the frosting while it is still in the mixing bowl. Remember to slowly build up the colour to the right shade. If you add too much colouring you cannot take it away.

### STEP 2

Beat the frosting on a medium speed for about 2 minutes until the colour is fully and evenly incorporated. Add more if necessary.

---

#### FURTHERING YOUR SKILLS

- If you need a really white frosting, choose the palest colour of butter you can find. Then, when you are beating the fat and sugar together, beat for 2 minutes longer. The longer you beat the frosting, the lighter in colour it will be.

- Remember, if you are using a liquid flavouring or colouring you may need to add a few extra tablespoons of icing sugar to correct the consistency of the frosting.

- The consistency of the mixture will change depending on how much icing sugar you use.

---

**EQUIPMENT**

*Colouring of your choice (see page 15)*

*Cocktail sticks*

# Modelling chocolate

Modelling chocolate is a great alternative to gum paste if you are working on a chocolate cake. Although it does not set as solid as gum paste, modelling chocolate holds its shape and is ideal for making roses, among other decorations. It is best to make the chocolate mixture 24 hours before using it.

**MAKES**
About 500 g (1 lb. 2 oz.) modelling chocolate (enough to make 20 roses, as described on page 138)

## INGREDIENTS

*450 g (1 lb.) white couverture chocolate, chopped, or use chocolate chips*

*7 tbsp. glucose syrup*

### STEP 1

Break the chocolate into a bowl and gently melt it in a double boiler or microwave (see pages 128–129). It is important that the chocolate doesn't become too warm. When it has melted about halfway, stir for one minute, then remove it from the heat source and continue to stir until completely melted. The chocolate will then be warm to the touch.

### STEP 2

Meanwhile, warm the glucose syrup in a saucepan over a gentle heat until it is just warm to the touch.

### STEP 3

Add the glucose syrup to the melted chocolate immediately, and stir with a silicone spatula until it is fully combined. It will start to thicken, so you need to work quickly.

### STEP 4

Transfer the mixture into an airtight container and let it sit at room temperature for 24 hours before using it.

### STEP 5

Remove a small amount of the modelling chocolate from the tub and work it between your hands until it becomes malleable and smooth.

> ### FURTHERING YOUR SKILLS
>
> **Your body heat will help to soften the modelling chocolate and make it easier to shape. If you find it is too soft, place it back into the airtight container and leave until it has returned to room temperature.**

# Chocolate ganache

A combination of chocolate and cream, ganache is the most indulgent form of cake covering. Ganache moulds to the shape of the cake, so it allows you to create sharp or decorative edges. I recommend buying couverture chocolate from specialty baking shops or online, with cocoa solids of above 55 percent. Avoid using normal chocolate (even if it is good quality) as supermarket brands have a low percentage of cocoa butter, which can lead to a lumpy result.

**MAKES**
450 g (1 lb.) ganache (enough to cover a 18 cm (7 in.) round cake or 12 cupcakes)

### INGREDIENTS

*225 ml (8 fl oz.) single cream*

*250 g (8 oz.) dark couverture chocolate, at least 55% cocoa solids, broken into very small pieces or use chocolate chips*

### STEP 1

Place the cream in a saucepan over a low heat and gently bring to the boil, stirring occasionally to prevent it from sticking to the bottom of the saucepan. As soon as it boils, remove the saucepan from the heat.

### STEP 2

Meanwhile, place the chocolate pieces or chips in a heatproof bowl. Pour the hot cream over the top. Use a whisk to stir the cream and chocolate gently. Keep whisking until the chocolate has fully melted and the consistency becomes thick.

### STEP 3

Let the ganache cool slightly so that it is just beginning to harden before you use it. If you are using it later, store it in a sealed container in the fridge and return it to room temperature before using it.

# Marshmallow fondant

I prefer to use marshmallow fondant for all of my cakes because it is so smooth and easy to work with. However, if you would like to work with a more traditional recipe, see the variation opposite. See pages 154–203 for skills and recipes that feature fondant.

**MAKES**
About 1 kg (2 lb. 4 oz.) fondant
(enough to cover a 18 cm (7 in.) round cake or 12 cupcakes)

**INGREDIENTS**

*500 g (1 lb. 2 oz.) plain white marshmallows*

*2 tbsp. boiled water, cooled*

*700 g (1 lb. 9 oz.) icing sugar, plus extra for dusting*

**STEP 1**
Put the marshmallows and water in a heatproof bowl and place the mixture in the microwave for about 90 seconds until the marshmallows double in size and become fluffy in appearance.

**STEP 2**
Stir the mixture thoroughly until the marshmallows melt and the mixture becomes silky and smooth.

**STEP 3**
At this point you can add a flavouring, such as vanilla extract, and a colouring of your choice (see page 15). Mix the marshmallow fondant, flavouring and colouring until the mixture is a solid colour.

**STEP 4**
Add the icing sugar, a little at a time, and mix thoroughly, until the mixture takes on the appearance of dough. You may find you do not need all of your icing sugar at this point.

5

# Traditional fondant

### STEP 5
Grease your hands and the work surface, and dust with a little icing sugar. Remove the dough from the bowl and start to knead it on your work surface until it becomes smooth and pliable.

### STEP 6
You can use your fondant right away or make it a few days in advance. If you decide to make it in advance, wrap it in cling film and store in an airtight container in a cool, dry place.

### STEP 1
Put the glucose syrup and glycerin in a heatproof bowl. Then sprinkle the gelatin over the top and add 1 tablespoon of water. Set aside for about 1 minute until the gelatin has swollen and softened.

### STEP 2
Place the bowl over a saucepan of hot water and stir it until the gelatin has dissolved.

### STEP 3
Place the icing sugar in a large mixing bowl and make a well in the centre. Then slowly pour the warmed gelatin liquid into the well, stirring constantly until the mixture has come together. Follow Steps 5 and 6 to finish making the fondant.

---

#### FURTHERING YOUR SKILLS

- If you find your fondant is getting a little dry, add a small amount of vegetable shortening and knead until it becomes smooth and pliable again.

- If your fondant becomes too warm and sticky, add a dusting of icing sugar and knead to remove the excess moisture.

---

#### INGREDIENTS

*125 ml (4 ½ fl oz.) glucose syrup*

*1 tbsp. glycerin*

*1 tbsp. unflavoured gelatin*

*900 g (2 lbs.) icing sugar, plus extra for dusting*

# Gum paste

I have used this easy recipe for all of the detailed decorations in this book. It is a high-quality recipe and can be made in smaller amounts when needed. See pages 204–249 for skills and recipes that feature gum paste. Always use within 24 hours of making, before the gum paste sets.

**MAKES**
About 250 g (9 oz.) gum paste (enough to make an average-sized figure)

1

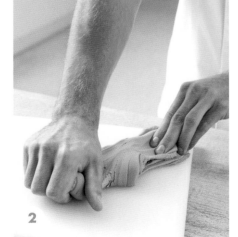

2

### STEP 1
Place the fondant and CMC powder on a clean work surface. Too much powder, and your gum paste will be too hard. Too little powder, and your paste will be too fragile to roll thinly and set properly.

### STEP 2
Knead together until the powder is fully incorporated into the fondant. The gum paste is ready to use immediately. Dainty items, such as lettering, will harden after approximately 15 minutes, but large figures may require up to 3 hours. For items such as shoes and posed figures, let your models dry for a minimum of 24 hours before trying to add them to any cake.

### STEP 3
To store leftover gum paste, wrap in cling film and keep in an airtight container at room temperature. Use within 24 hours.

### INGREDIENTS
¼ quantity fondant (see page 34)

1 tsp. CMC powder

## FURTHERING YOUR SKILLS
If you find the paste sticking as you are kneading it, use a light dusting of corn flour or icing sugar on the work surface to keep it from sticking.

# Marzipan for modelling

Marzipan is a great material to model. When you use it with CMC powder it will firm up in much the same way as gum paste. One thing to remember is that the models will not be as strong as those made with regular gum paste. See pages 250–271 for skills and recipes that feature marzipan.

1

3

**MAKES**
250 g (9 oz.) modelling marzipan

### STEP 1
Add colours or flavours to your marzipan if desired (see page 38). Place the marzipan and CMC powder on a clean work surface and knead together until the ingredients are fully incorporated.

### STEP 2
If the marzipan becomes too moist, use a little icing sugar to bring it back to the right consistency.

### STEP 3
The marzipan modelling paste is ready to use immediately. Dainty items, such as lettering, will harden after approximately 15 minutes, but large figures may require up to 3 hours. For items such as shoes and posed figures, let your models dry for a minimum of 24 hours before trying to add them to any cake.

### STEP 4
To store leftover marzipan, wrap in cling film and keep in an airtight container at room temperature – use within 24 hours.

### INGREDIENTS

*250 g (9 oz.) marzipan*

*1 tsp. CMC powder*

# Colouring fondant, gum paste and marzipan

You can buy pre-treated fondant in various colours, but it is more fun and versatile to make your own. This means you will have a large variety of fondant and gum paste shades to choose from, as you learn to create your own signature colours. The process for colouring is the same for fondant, gum paste and marzipan. Remember to add colouring paste sparingly – a little goes a long way.

**EQUIPMENT**

*Food colourings of your choice*

*Cocktail sticks*

1

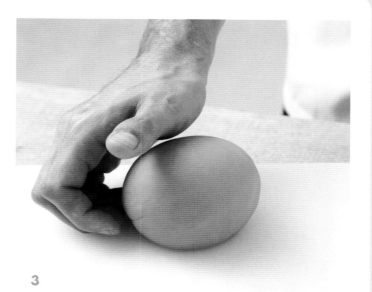

3

2

## STEP 1

Apply the food colouring to the fondant, gum paste or marzipan using a cocktail stick, in very small amounts at a time. It is important to build the colour slowly.

## STEP 2

Knead the colouring through, adding more if necessary, until it becomes a solid single colour with no streaks.

## STEP 3

Wrap your fondant, gum paste or marzipan well in cling film and then store in an airtight container until needed.

### FURTHERING YOUR SKILLS

- I find that shop-bought fondant in bright colours is the best base for darker, stronger colours as it saves time and uses less food colouring.

- I always use the rule of 'less is more' when colouring. You can always add more if needed, but if you start with too much it is much harder to rectify.

- Colours develop over a few hours, so it is best to colour your fondant, gum paste or marzipan the day before to get an accurate idea of the colour you have made. You can always adjust it if you need to.

- If the colour you made is too dark, add a little white fondant or marzipan and knead until both of the colours are blended. If you need to, you can add more of the white fondant or marzipan until you get the colour you are looking for.

# Royal icing

This type of icing is great for piping into intricate designs because it sets firm and holds its shape. Royal icing also works well as edible glue if you don't have your own edible glue on hand (see page 41). See pages 272–285 for skills and recipes that feature royal icing.

**MAKES**

About 250 g (9 oz.) royal icing

### STEP 1

Place the egg white in a very clean bowl of an electric stand mixer. Insert the whisk attachment and whisk until soft peaks form.

### STEP 2

Slowly spoon in the icing sugar, a little at a time, and keep whisking until you have added all of the sugar. The mixture should now be glossy and form a stiff peak but without being too grainy or powdery.

### STEP 3

Add the lemon juice and whisk for another minute. Now your royal icing will be ready to pipe. Use immediately, or the icing will dry out and harden too much to pipe.

### INGREDIENTS

*1 large egg white at room temperature*

*225 g (8 oz.) icing sugar, sieved*

*1 tsp. lemon juice*

### FURTHERING YOUR SKILLS

Use an electric stand mixer to make this icing. It will make it a lot easier when adding the icing sugar and will give better results.

# Edible glue

This amount of glue will go a long way, but it is difficult to make in smaller quantities. Make the glue the day before you want to use it, and store in the fridge in a sealed container. It will keep for up to 2 weeks. When applied, the glue takes a few minutes to become tacky and then dries quickly.

### STEP 1

Place the CMC power and water into a small bowl and mix together well with a teaspoon. Do not worry if the mixture is not blending well, it will come together overnight.

### STEP 2

Transfer the mixture to a storage container with a lid and leave in the fridge overnight.

### STEP 3

The next day, remove the container from the fridge and stir the glue. It should be clear with a thick dropping consistency. If it is too thick to paint with easily, add a drop or two of water and mix together well.

### INGREDIENTS

2 tbsp. boiled water, left to cool slightly

1/4 tsp. CMC powder

### FURTHERING YOUR SKILLS

This glue will not stick immediately, so set aside glued items for at least a couple of hours to achieve the desired result.

# Preparing and covering cakes

Preparation is a very important part of cake decorating. Good planning and solid construction are essential to your design. With good construction and preparation you will find it easier to achieve the finished look that you dream of. Think of preparing a cake as similar to building a house. Without a good foundation the whole house will fall in on itself and the same goes for cake making. If you use the wrong type of cake or construct it without it being level, then your finished product will collapse.

# Greasing and flouring a cake tin

It is always best to use a springform cake tin when baking cakes, as it is much easier to release the cake once it is cooked. It is necessary to grease the tin to keep the cake from sticking to it. You want to create a non-stick layer between the tin and the cake.

### STEP 1

Allow the butter to reach room temperature or gently melt it in a saucepan.

### STEP 2

Use parchment paper, or a pastry brush if you melted the butter, to spread the butter all over the inside of the cake tin. Make sure all surfaces are evenly coated. You can check this by holding the cake tin up to the light and checking for any areas that are not shiny.

### STEP 3

Sprinkle the tin's surface with an even coating of flour. Then tap gently and tip the tin to remove any excess flour.

## EQUIPMENT

*Cake tin*

*1 tbsp. butter*

*Flour*

## FURTHERING YOUR SKILLS

You can also use a pastry brush to spread the flour around the inside of the tin. This will help keep your work area clean. If you move the flour all around the tin it will get on your worktop.

# Lining a cake tin

This technique will allow you to glide your cake out of the tin with ease.

## FURTHERING YOUR SKILLS

- Greasing the base of the tin before putting the paper in keeps it from moving around when you add the batter.

- If you are using an unusual shaped cake tin, such as a giant cupcake tin, it is easiest to coat it with a thin layer of a cake release spray rather than line the whole tin.

## EQUIPMENT

*Cake tin*

*Parchment paper*

*Pencil*

*Scissors*

### STEP 1

For springform cake tins, put a sheet of parchment paper over the base, then put the ring over it and close. Trim around the edges.

### STEP 2

For fixed base tins, draw around the base of the tin onto the parchment paper, cut this out, then put it on the greased base of the tin.

### STEP 3

To line the sides of a tin, cut parchment paper 2.5 cm (1 in.) longer than the circumference and 7.5 cm (3 in.) higher than the depth. Fold it down 2.5 cm (1 in.) from the top and cut incisions all the way around the tin. With the incisions at the base, place this around the inside of the greased tin before adding the base lining.

### STEP 4

For a square tin, measure the width and length of the tin and add twice the depth. Cut parchment paper this size. Place the tin in the middle of the paper and make four cuts to the corners of the tin. Press into the greased tin overlapping the edges.

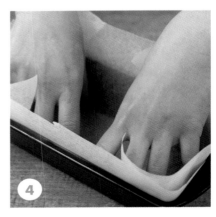

# Testing a cake for doneness

Learning this essential skill will save you from turning out an overdone or underdone cake.

### STEP 1
If the cake is cooked through, it will spring back to your touch.

### STEP 2
Or you could insert a cocktail stick or skewer into the centre of the cake. If it comes out clean, it is fully cooked. If the cake is not fully cooked, put it back into the oven for 5 more minutes.

## EQUIPMENT

*Cocktail stick or skewer*

### FURTHERING YOUR SKILLS
Ovens can vary, which means that cooking times will also vary. So keep a close eye on cakes when they are almost done. As you bake more cakes, you will learn more about your oven and you will be able to judge whether to leave the cake in for a few minutes longer, or whether to take it out a few minutes earlier.

# Turning out and cooling a cake

If you have gone to the effort of baking a delicious homemade cake, you should learn the correct way to turn it out perfectly.

**STEP 1**

Carefully, run your knife around the inside of the cake tin. Keep the edge of the knife against the tin at all times. You do not want to cut into the cake.

**STEP 2**

Release the ring from the base.

**STEP 3**

Now slide the cake (on the parchment paper) onto a cooling rack. Once it is cool enough to handle, you can remove the parchment paper and allow to cool fully.

---

## EQUIPMENT

*Table knife*

*Wire cooling rack*

*Parchment paper*

---

### FURTHERING YOUR SKILLS

- To remove a cake from a loose bottomed cake tin, place a jar on the work surface and put the cake tin on top, gently easing the sides downwards. Then transfer the cake to the cooling rack.

# Levelling a cake

Making sure your cake is level is important, especially if you intend to stack further layers on top. Before you cover your cake, you will need to level each layer.

### STEP 1
Place the cake on a cake board and set the cake wire to the desired height.

### STEP 2
Set the cake wire to the desired height, while keeping both of the wire's feet on the table. Use a sawing motion to cut through the cake, leaving you with a perfectly level layer.

### STEP 3
Repeat this method for each layer.

### EQUIPMENT

*Cake board*

*Cake wire*

# Carving a cake

You can carve almost anything out of cake and if you cannot carve it entirely, you can create the main body to build upon. Deciding on the cake you want to use for carving is really important. A light and fluffy cake will most likely crumble when you start to carve it. However, a Madeira cake (see page 24) is ideal for carving because it can take on on almost any shape.

**EQUIPMENT**

*Sharp knife*

*Turntable*

### STEP 1
When carving a cake, use a sharp knife to avoid excess friction on the cake surface. Make sure you know where to begin carving to create your chosen design.

### STEP 2
Remember that you cannot attach cake as easily as you can remove it, so make your alterations a little at a time to avoid any big mistakes.

### STEP 3
When you are carving a cake that needs to be symmetrical, be sure to check your carving intermittently. You can do this by getting down to the same level as the cake to see if you have carved the cake evenly.

# Filling and crumb coating a cake

Once you have levelled your cake, you will need to fill and cover it with frosting, so it forms a solid structure before adding any fondant or marzipan to it. The frosting also gives the fondant something to adhere to.

## EQUIPMENT

*Cake card of the same dimension as the cake*

*Palette knife*

*Spirit level*

*Turntable*

*Non-slip matting*

*Cake board*

*Metal scraper*

## STEP 1

To fill the cake, place the base layer on a cake card of the same size. For extra stability, you may wish to use a small amount of frosting or royal icing as glue to attach the cake to the card. For cakes of more than one tier, you only need a cake card for the bottom tier.

## STEP 2

Coat the top of the base layer with the frosting using a palette knife. Place the next layer of cake on top and repeat these steps with any additional layers.

## STEP 3

Once you have stacked the layers, run your fingertip around the edge of the cake where it is joined, to remove any frosting that has escaped.

## STEP 4

Use a spirit level to check that your cake is perfectly level and adjust as needed. An easy way to do this is to insert the palette knife between the layers and lift it slightly to even out the cake.

### STEP 5

Chill the cake for 30 minutes in the fridge until the filling has set. This will help you when crumb coating the cake.

### STEP 6

Remove the cake from the fridge to prepare for frosting, stack the turntable, non-slip mat, cake board, cake card and cake, respectively.

### STEP 7

Use the palette knife to spread frosting all around the sides of the cake, turning the turntable as you work.

### STEP 8

Using the metal scraper with the bottom edge flat on the base board and the side straight against the edge of the cake, turn the turntable continuously until you have a smooth vertical side to the cake. If the cake is not yet flat, wipe away the excess from the scraper and repeat until the frosting is smooth.

### STEP 9

Apply a small amount of the frosting to the top of the cake with the palette knife and smooth it out using the scraper. Use gentle inward strokes to guide the excess frosting to the centre, which you can remove and smooth with the palette knife.

---

#### FURTHERING YOUR SKILLS

- If your turntable is only slightly bigger than the cake, try using a larger cake card or metal disc under the cake to make covering the cake easier. The removable bottom from a cake tin is ideal.

- For cakes that are made of more than one tier, coat the bottom tier on the cake board then remove the cake board, with the cake, from the turntable and repeat the process until you have stacked all of the layers. Some cakes require a fondant coating to strengthen them before stacking.

# Rolling out fondant and marzipan

Fondant and marzipan make perfect cake coverings and they are so simple to use. Most of the cakes and cake boards in this book are covered with fondant. I refer to fondant only in this skill, but marzipan and fondant can be rolled out and used in exactly the same way.

**EQUIPMENT**

*Icing spacers*

*Rolling pin*

### FURTHERING YOUR SKILLS

• If you are using marzipan and it is sticking to the work surface, use icing sugar rather than corn flour to dust.

• Keep your cake nearby while you are working with your fondant. Fondant will tear easily and you do not want to have to walk across the room to place it on the cake.

## STEP 1

Before rolling out the fondant, knead it well until the consistency is pliable and stretchy. If you try to roll out the fondant before it is ready, it will crack when you lay it over the cake.

## STEP 2

If you find the fondant is sticking to your work surface when you roll it out, sprinkle a light dusting of corn flour on the surface (or icing sugar if rolling out marzipan).

## STEP 3

Roll back and forth with an even pressure on the rolling pin. Use spacers to help roll the rolling pin along. This will help to ensure the fondant is the same thickness across the whole piece.

## STEP 4

When you need to move the fondant onto a cake board or to cover a cake, place the rolling pin in the centre of the fondant and gently lift the fondant up and over the rolling pin. The rolling pin will support the fondant as you lift it up and place it on the surface.

# Covering a cake board

A cake is not complete without a perfectly covered cake board. This is an easy technique and will give your cakes a professional look. You can also cover the board with marzipan instead of fondant.

## EQUIPMENT

Cake board

Icing smoother

Double-sided tape

Ribbon

Spray bottle with water

### FURTHERING YOUR SKILLS

When choosing ribbons, remember to measure about 3 mm ($\frac{1}{8}$ in.) above the depth of your board, so that you will have the right width of ribbon to cover both the board and fondant layer.

**STEP 1**
Prepare and roll out the fondant to about 3 mm ($\frac{1}{8}$ in.) thick. Make sure it is large enough to cover the cake board (see pages 54–55).

**STEP 2**
Before you place the fondant over the board, give the board a quick spray with water to help it stick.

**STEP 3**
Fold the fondant back toward you and over the rolling pin, and then carefully lift the fondant up and onto the cake board.

**STEP 4**
Use the icing smoothers to affix the fondant to the board, carefully smoothing out any air bubbles, to create a flat surface. Keep the icing smoother parallel to the cake board so that you do not dent the fondant. Work from the centre outwards.

**STEP 5**
Lift the cake board and, using a sharp knife, trim away any excess fondant.

**STEP 6**
Trim the board with a ribbon of your choice using double-sided tape.

# Covering a cake

You can use fondant or marzipan to cover an entire cake. If you decide to use a fondant finish, you can put a layer of marzipan underneath. Whether your cake is round, square or a more complicated shape, these tips will help you get the smoothest finish possible. I refer to fondant throughout this skill as most of the covered cakes in this book use fondant, however if you are using marzipan, the same techniques apply.

**EQUIPMENT**

*Icing spacers*

*Icing smoother*

*Rolling pin*

## FURTHERING YOUR SKILLS

- When working with marzipan, always use icing sugar, never corn flour, to dust work surfaces and tools. Over time, corn flour reacts with marzipan and causes it to ferment.

- Covering a cake that is an irregular shape can seem daunting. Take your time and remember not to put too much pressure on the fondant.

- When covering irregular shapes, make sure you have rolled the fondant out large enough to cover the cake. It is much harder to peel off fondant and rescue it than you realise.

**STEP 1**
Prepare and roll out the fondant to the required size and thickness (see pages 54–55).

**STEP 2**
Place the rolling pin in the centre of the fondant and gently lift the fondant up and over the rolling pin. The rolling pin will then support the fondant as you lift it up and onto the surface of the cake.

**STEP 3**
Press the fondant into the sides of the cake, then use upward sweeping hand motions to smooth it out. If you are working on a square cake, you will need to start placing the corners of the cake before you work around

to the sides. This is to ensure that the fondant does not pucker. Once it is all smoothed out, remove the excess from the corners and base of the cake using a sharp knife.

**STEP 4**
Use the icing smoother to smooth the sides and the top of the cake, using a back and forth motion. Finally, trim away the excess from the bottom edge.

# Covering a cake with ganache

Ganache is a luxurious covering for cakes and sets firm. It can be used as a covering or as a base to lay fondant over. The recipe for ganache is given on page 32 and the quantity is suitable for covering an 18 cm (7 in.) round, basic sponge cake.

## EQUIPMENT

*Turntable*

*Non-slip matting*

*Cake board*

*Palette knife*

*Metal scraper*

## STEP 1
Fill and crumb coat your cake (see page 50).

## STEP 2
Remove the cake from the fridge and stack the turntable, non-slip mat, cake board and cake, respectively.

## STEP 3
Use the palette knife to spread ganache all around the side of the cake, turning the turntable as you work. There is no need to coat the top at this stage.

## STEP 4
Using the metal scraper with the bottom edge flat on the base board and the side straight against the edge of

the cake, turn the turntable continuously until you have a smooth vertical side to the cake. If the cake is not yet flat, wipe away the excess from the scraper and repeat until the ganache is smooth.

## STEP 5
Spread a small amount of the ganache onto the top of the cake with the palette knife and smooth it out with the scraper. Use gentle inward strokes to guide the excess ganache to the centre, which you can remove and smooth with the spatula.

## STEP 6
Let the cake set overnight before decorating it. If you are short on time, you can freeze it for 8–10 minutes, but no longer.

# Dowelling a cake

To make a tiered cake you will need to stack one cake on top of another. You will need to use the 'dowelling' method to do this. The way this method works is you will insert small structural supports to the base layer to hold the tier above it. I would suggest using wooden dowels if you are stacking more than two cakes. In this example, I use jumbo straws because they provide enough support for two layers.

**EQUIPMENT**

*Cake cards, the same size as each tier of cake*

*Spirit level*

*Jumbo straws*

*Palette knife*

### STEP 1

Frost each tier separately as described in the recipe you are following, and use a little royal icing to stick the bottom tier to a cake card that is the same size as the cake.

### STEP 2

Using a spirit level, even out each tier of the cake (see page 48).

### STEP 3

Take a cake card that is the same size as the top layer, and gently press it into the surface of the bottom layer. This will leave a light imprint on the surface, which gives you an idea of where the straws should go.

### STEP 4

Insert one of the straws into the cake, take care to place it straight down into the cake board and not at an angle, or it will not provide any support.

### STEP 5

Put a knife mark on the dowel where the top of the cake hits, then pull the straw out. You will be using the straw as a spacer between the two cakes.

### STEP 6

Cut on the knife mark to the correct length, then repeat the process with the other straws. For a circular cake, you will need 6–8 straws. For a square cake, you will need 8–12 straws.

### STEP 7
Place all of the straws 3 cm (1 ¼ in.) inside the imprint you have made.

### STEP 8
Lay a cake board on top of the straws and use the spirit level to check that you have created a level base for the next tier.

### STEP 9
Once you are happy with the way it looks, spread a thin layer of royal icing across the top of the bottom tier.

### STEP 10
Use a palette knife to carefully position the next tier into place. Repeat this process for each tier.

### FURTHERING YOUR SKILLS
Wait until the fondant has fully set on the cake before you stack the tiers. This will make the stacking process easier and will prevent any accidental dents in the fondant.

# Flat topping a cupcake

Flat topping a cupcake is the most common method used for covering a cupcake with frosting and fondant. It provides the base for adding decoration, or for embellishing the cake with edible paints or glitters. This method is used as the basis for many of the cupcake projects throughout this book.

## EQUIPMENT

*Small knife*

*Palette knife*

*Rolling pin*

*Circle cutter*

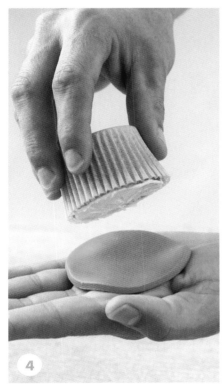

**STEP 1**

If the top of your cupcake isn't flat, level it using a small sharp knife. Use the palette knife to spread a thin layer of the frosting across the top of each cupcake. Cup the cupcake case with your hand to prevent the case from peeling as you sweep against it with the knife. Be sure to wipe away any excess frosting from the edge of the cake.

**STEP 2**

Once the frosting is level, roll out a walnut-sized piece of fondant until it is 3 mm (1/8 in.) thick.

**STEP 3**

Use a circle cutter that is 1 cm (1/2 in.) larger than the top of the cupcake and cut out a circle of fondant.

**STEP 4**

Place the circle upside down in your hand and the cupcake topside down onto the disc.

**STEP 5**

Make sure the cupcake is in the centre before flipping it over.

**STEP 6**

Using your finger, smooth the edges of the fondant down, turning the cupcake as you work. This will leave you with a neat finish and it will seal in the cupcake and keep it fresher longer.

# Making a candy melt shell

Candy melt shells are a fun and versatile way to present your cakes. Giant cupcakes are incredibly popular at the moment and make great centrepieces for birthday parties. With the help of my instructions, you will be able to make a candy shell as the base of your giant cupcake. This will give the cupcake a truly whimsical appearance.

**EQUIPMENT**

*Giant cupcake mould*

*Spatula*

*Sharp knife*

**INGREDIENTS**

*350 g (12 oz.) candy melts*

### STEP 1
Melt the candies as described on page 128.

### STEP 2
Pour one-third of the mixture into the base of the giant cupcake mould. Using a spatula, smooth the mixture up the sides of the mould. At this point, you will have a thin coating around the base. Do not worry if you can see through some areas, as they will be covered later.

### STEP 3
Place the mould in the fridge for 30 minutes or until the shell is firm to the touch.

### STEP 4
Remove the mould from the fridge and repeat the coating again using the remaining half of the mixture. The chocolate will not be neat or smooth inside. Once you are finished, the outside will be perfect and the inside will be covered with cake, so no one will notice it.

### STEP 5
Place the mould back in the fridge for another 30 minutes or it until it is firm.

### STEP 6
Repeat the coating one last time, then chill it until it is solid.

### STEP 7
Once fully chilled, remove the mould from the fridge, give the bottom of the mould a good tap and the shell should immediately pop out onto the work surface.

### STEP 8
Using a sharp knife, level the top edge of the candy melt shell.

---

**FURTHERING YOUR SKILLS**

If the shell begins to crack when you remove it from the mould, put it back in the mould. Give it another coating of candy melts to cover the cracks and chill again.

# Working with frosting

Frosting is everyone's favourite when it comes to cake toppings. The creamy texture and sweet taste appeals to people of all ages. It is often the first thing children will go for at a party. This chapter guides you through a comprehensive list of frosting skills that will help you through the recipes in this chapter and encourage you to try designing your own frostings. For the basic frosting recipe, see page 28.

# Piping techniques

Piping techniques are easy to learn and help you greatly when it comes to designing your own cakes and cupcakes. From embellishments to fully covered cakes, you can add as little, or as much, frosting detailing as you like. The beauty of frosting is that if you go wrong, you can always just wipe the mistake away and start again. Frosting is a great medium for beginners.

## Filling a piping bag

When I began baking and decorating cakes, filling a piping bag was the one technique I struggled with. Then I learned this fine technique that made it much easier.

**STEP 1**
Take a tall glass measuring jug or a vase that is big enough to hold the piping bag. Place your piping bag, with the tip already attached, into the vase and fold the open end of the piping bag out and over the top edge of the vase. I always start with half of the piping bag over the edge of the vase, to get the frosting down into the tip of the bag.

**STEP 2**
Use a spatula or knife to get the frosting into the bag. Make sure to push out any air that may have gotten into the bag. This can ruin your piping technique.

**STEP 3**
If you get bubbles in the bag, don't worry. Once the bag is filled, pinch the bubbles through the bag and squeeze the air upwards so it releases. Then proceed to squeeze more frosting into the space where the air was.

### EQUIPMENT

Piping bag

Tip of your choice

Glass measuring jug or vase

### FURTHERING YOUR SKILLS

The glass measuring jug or vase also makes a great resting place for the piping bag if you need to stop at any point.

# Holding a piping bag

Do not let piping bags strike fear into you, all it takes is practise. When you are piping frosting, use a bag that you feel comfortable holding in one hand. You have probably seen many baking shows on television that show pastry chefs and bakers using huge piping bags, which they throw over their shoulder. Remember that these people are professionals and this is required in their trade to work efficiently.

**STEP 1**
To hold your piping bag, push all of the frosting down to the tip and fold the top sides of the bag into the centre.

**STEP 2**
Hold the bag in one hand, just above the frosting, using your thumb and forefinger and then use your other hand to twist the bag to create pressure on the frosting.

## FURTHERING YOUR SKILLS

An average-sized piping bag is perfectly adequate for any of the recipes in this book. Once you feel comfortable with this size, you may choose to gradually build up to larger sizes.

# Starting to pipe

It is a misconception that once you begin to pipe, you need to apply pressure to attach the frosting to the cake. Really, the frosting is so moist that once it touches the cake's surface, it adheres on its own. However, it is important to give the piping tip room to move, so hold it just above the cake surface.

## STEP 1

Your starting place will depend on which piping technique you have chosen to use, the simplest techniques start at the centre working towards the outer edge. Start frosting at a comfortable pace, applying a constant pressure on the frosting in the bag at all times. You must apply constant pressure to keep the frosting regular and consistent.

## STEP 2

When you are piping, adjust the bag often to keep the frosting moving through the bag. This will help you keep the frosting consistent and you will work faster too.

## EQUIPMENT

*Piping bag*

*Tip of your choice*

# Finishing neatly when piping

*Now that you have piped the perfect swirl, you say to yourself, I really do not want to mess this up. Do not worry. I will help you bring your whole design together.*

**STEP 1**

When you have finished piping, stop squeezing the bag and lift it away from the cupcake.

**STEP 2**

If your frosting is super smooth, you may find that lifting away the piping tip creates a small tail on the piped shape. If this happens, you can use a damp paintbrush to gently push the frosting back down.

## FURTHERING YOUR SKILLS

- When you are piping ruffles with frosting, the finishing technique is slightly different because you want to hide where the frosting ends. Once you get to the end of your design, point the piping tip down towards the cake, then stop squeezing and lift away. You should find the frosting ends out of sight. If you create any kind of tail, do as I suggested above and use a damp paintbrush to rectify it.

- Use warm, soapy water to clean your paintbrushes. Make sure you dry them well and store them upright in a glass to avoid damaging the bristles.

## EQUIPMENT

*Piping bag*

*Tip of your choice*

*Paintbrush (optional)*

# Piping a simple swirl

Before you progress
to piping intricate swirls
and flowers, it is important
to master the perfect
plain swirl.

**USING THIS SKILL**
Classic Swirl Cupcakes: page 98

## EQUIPMENT

*Piping bag*

*Wilton No. 1A round decorating tip*

### STEP 1
Secure the tip in your piping bag, then fill it with your chosen frosting (see page 74).

### STEP 2
Start with a central, single, squeeze of frosting, which will create a core for the swirl so that it does not fall in on itself. Hold the bag vertically and squeeze it until you get the right amount of frosting. Then stop squeezing and lift away from the cupcake.

### STEP 3
Move to the edge and begin to pipe around the edge of the cupcake.

### STEP 4
Once you have piped a complete circle, without stopping, move inwards and continue to pipe in a spiral up and over the central core.

### STEP 5
When you reach the centre of the swirl, stop squeezing and lift away.

# Piping a twisted swirl

This swirl is incredibly popular because it reminds people of the way ice cream looks. It is easy to do and it will soon become your favourite skill. I have described how to make this swirl on a cupcake, but you can also pipe them all over the top of a larger cake.

## EQUIPMENT

*Piping bag*

*Wilton No. 1 open star or No. 2D drop flower piping tip*

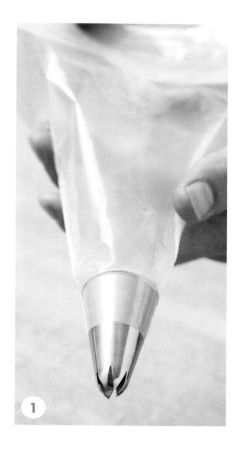

### STEP 1

Secure the tip in your piping bag, then fill it with your chosen frosting (see page 74).

### STEP 2

Start with a central single squeeze of frosting, which will create the core for the swirl so that it does not fall in on itself. Hold the bag vertically and squeeze it until the twisted swirl is of the desired size, then stop squeezing and lift away from the cupcake.

### STEP 3

Move to the edge and begin to pipe around the edge of the cupcake.

### STEP 4

Once you have piped a complete circle, without stopping, move inwards and continue to pipe in a spiral up and over the central core of the cupcake.

### STEP 5

When you reach the centre of the swirl, stop squeezing and lift away.

# Piping a rose swirl

This type of decoration is simple but effective. It looks more intricate than it is. You can achieve it easily with the right equipment.

**USING THIS SKILL**
Rose Swirl Cupcakes: page 104

## EQUIPMENT

*Palette knife*

*Piping bag*

*Wilton No. 2D drop flower piping tip*

## FURTHERING YOUR SKILLS

**Add two colours of frosting to your piping bag, side by side. This will give your roses a two-toned effect.**

## STEP 1
Secure the tip in your piping bag, then fill it with your chosen frosting (see page 74).

## STEP 2
Spread a layer of frosting over the cake's surface using a palette knife. Holding the piping bag vertically, so the tip is pointing directly down as you pipe, start at the centre of the cake and pipe in a tight circle to create the rosebud centre.

## STEP 3
Slowly moving outwards and piping in a spiral, continue until you have made the size of rose swirl you are aiming for. As you pipe the rose, keep the tip about 3 cm (1 ¼ in.) above the cake. The frosting will fall into place and attach itself to the flat layer of frosting beneath. If you pipe too close to the cake, you will find the tip will drag through the frosting beneath, leaving you with broken lines. Stop squeezing and lift your piping tip away from the cake.

## STEP 4
Add a small edible decoration to hide the end of your piping.

# Piping a rosette

A rosette is both incredibly pretty and easy to create. This technique can be incorporated into many different themes and types of cakes.

**USING THIS SKILL**
Rosette Cupcakes: page 106

## EQUIPMENT

*Piping bag*

*PME FT070 piping tip*

## FURTHERING YOUR SKILLS

When piping with this tip, the slower you move your hand around the cake the more ruffles you will achieve. Conversely, the faster you move, the fewer ruffles you will have.

### STEP 1

Secure the tip in your piping bag, then fill it with your chosen frosting (see page 74).

### STEP 2

When piping a rosette, bear in mind that the opening of this particular tip is along its side. Therefore, you will need to keep the opening of the tip pointing directly parallel to the surface of the cupcake. Begin by piping a circle around the edge of the cupcake or about 5 cm (2 in.) in diameter. As you squeeze the piping bag, the frosting will ruffle itself.

### STEP 3

Once you have completed the circle of frosting, keep squeezing and lift away from the cake while moving towards the centre of the cupcake. This will stop the frosting from creating a tail that sticks out of the design.

### STEP 4

Pipe a second circle of ruffles in the centre of the first circle to sit on top of the first.

# Piping teardrops

Have you ever walked into a high-end bakery and thought about how elegant the cupcakes look? I will teach you how to achieve that elegant look using the 'teardrop effect'. It is a classic design that will never go out of style.

**EQUIPMENT**

*Piping bag*

*Wilton No. 1A round decorating tip*

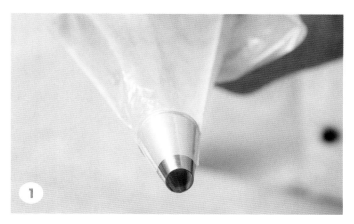

**STEP 1**

Secure the tip in your piping bag, then fill it with your chosen frosting (see page 74).

**STEP 2**

Hold the piping bag vertically over the cake, with the tip directly over the centre of the cupcake, about 1 cm (½ in.) from the surface. Gently squeeze the piping bag so that the frosting forms a large ball.

**STEP 3**

Continue squeezing until you are happy with the size of the ball of frosting, then stop squeezing and lift up the bag at the same time. You will create a tail of frosting pointing upwards, that is known as the 'teardrop effect'.

**STEP 4**

Repeat to cover the surface of the cake and finish with small edible decorations.

# Texturising frosting

Texturising can be a hard skill to master. This technique will require you to ignore everything you have learned. Although you have spent a lot of time being precise, this technique asks that you take some risks. To add texture to your frosting, you can use almost any tool. The round tip of a paintbrush, a palette knife and a texture comb can all be used to create great texture. The options are endless.

**USING THIS SKILL**
Rustic Textured Cake: page 114

## EQUIPMENT

*Piping bag and tip*

*Object for texturising, such as a palette knife, ruler or texture comb*

*Turntable (optional)*

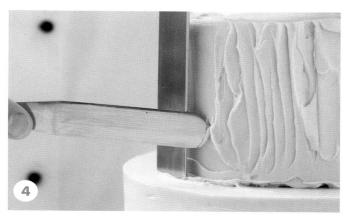

### STEP 1

Apply a thick layer of frosting to the cake. Aim for a coating of around 3 cm (1 ¼ in.). Keep in mind, it will not stay this thick once you have finished texturising.

### STEP 2

To create a random texture on your frosting, use a palette knife to make arching movements in all different directions. Switch the hands you hold the spatula with. This will create varying amounts of pressure for a more random effect.

### STEP 3

Continue to look back at the cake, from a distance, as you work. Move back with a small amount of frosting on your spatula. Spread it onto the cake before adjusting the pattern of the frosting. This is so you do not break through to the cake.

### STEP 4

You can make texture on stripes by running your tool against a ruler. This is a sure way to maintain a clean stripe.

# Creating a fur effect

It may seem challenging to create furry little monster cakes that children will love. I can assure you that it is not with a multi-opening decorating tip. You can easily create the effect of fur – no one will know that you did not pipe every single strand individually.

**USING THIS SKILL**
Furry Monster Cupcakes: page 110

### STEP 1
Secure the tip in your piping bag, then fill it with your chosen frosting. This particular tip has many small holes, which creates the fur effect.

### STEP 2
Hold the piping tip directly over the cake about 3 mm (⅛ in.) away from the cake's surface. Squeeze the bag and lift away, from the cake, to get the effect of fur.

### STEP 3
Repeat Step 2 until the entire top of the cake is covered. You may choose to finish with fondant eyes.

---

**EQUIPMENT**

*Piping bag*

*Wilton No. 233 multi-opening decorating tip*

---

**FURTHERING YOUR SKILLS**

When you are piping, how fast you pull your hand away determines the length of the strand of frosting. Try using different speeds until you find the style that suits you.

# Piping a grass effect

This technique is ideal for garden or sport-themed cupcakes. You will have so much fun once you have perfected this technique. To get the effect of grass, you need a piping tip with multiple openings at the end.

**USING THIS SKILL**
Grass Effect Cupcakes: page 112

### STEP 1
Secure the tip in your piping bag and then fill it with green coloured frosting.

### STEP 2
Cover the area you want to pipe with a layer of the green frosting and spread it with your spatula. This will help to seal the cake and hide any gaps between the grass.

### STEP 3
Hold your piping bag vertically, with the tip slightly above the surface. Squeeze the bag; as the frosting adheres to the cake, gently raise it up and release your squeeze. Repeat this process across the surface of the cake.

### EQUIPMENT

*Piping bag*

*Wilton No. 233 multi-opening decorating tip*

*Palette knife*

### FURTHERING YOUR SKILLS

For a garden-themed cake, you can use this method to pipe reeds around a pond. It also works particularly well with larger cakes, to hide where the cake meets the board.

# Piping horizontal ruffles

This technique leaves you with a cake that looks like it has been coated in many layers of frosting. The ruffles give the cake an incredibly pretty look and can be added to almost any design.

**USING THIS SKILL**
Layered Cake: page 118

## EQUIPMENT

*Piping bag*

*PME FT070 piping tip*

## FURTHERING YOUR SKILLS

- If your hand gets tired from squeezing the bag, lift the bag away and adjust it, then go back to the exact same point and continue piping. The ruffle is a very forgiving decoration so you will not notice where it breaks.

- If the edges do not ruffle out enough for you, let the frosting set for 30 minutes, then take a dampened paintbrush and gently tease the edges out more. Make sure you let the frosting sit for long enough because it can easily tear. Test out the frosting on the back of the cake first, to make sure it is ready. You do not want to ruin the effect of the cake.

### STEP 1
Secure the tip in your piping bag, then fill it with your chosen frosting (see page 74).

### STEP 2
Starting at the top of the cake, make sure you hold the piping tip with the wider end at the bottom and the thin end at the top. Hold your tip at an angle so only the thicker edge of the frosting sticks to the cake.

### STEP 3
Pipe a single strip around the side of the cake. You are looking for the bottom edge of the ruffle to stick to the cake, but the top edge should stand just above the edge of the cake.

### STEP 4
Repeat Step 3, each time piping a strip 1 cm (½ in.) further down the side of the cake until covered. Each new ruffle slightly overlaps the one above. Try to start and finish at the same point. As you move down the cake, you will need to increase the angle that you hold the bag so the frosting sticks with just the thicker edge.

# Piping vertical ruffles

Piping vertically is tricky because you are holding your hands in an uncomfortable position. Remember, if you make a mistake, you can always start again. Follow these steps and you will master the technique in no time.

**USING THIS SKILL**
Vertical Ruffles and Pearls Cake:
page 120

## EQUIPMENT

*Piping bag*

*PME FT070 piping tip*

*Paintbrush (optional)*

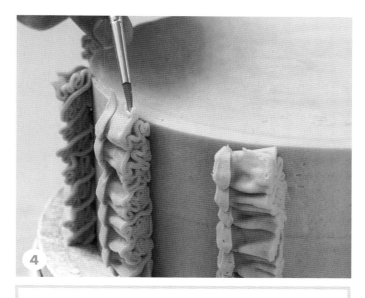

### FURTHERING YOUR SKILLS

- For this design, it is easier if you raise up the cake on a tall turntable or box.

- Remember, if all else fails, you can smooth the frosting away and start again to cover up any mistakes.

## STEP 1
Secure the tip in your piping bag, then fill it with your chosen frosting (see page 74).

## STEP 2
With the opening of the piping tip facing the side of the cake, start at the bottom edge and horizontal to the cake board. Squeeze, using constant pressure, as you move up the side of the cake.

## STEP 3
The frosting will naturally ruffle using this piping tip. Remember to use a steady and constant speed when you are moving up the side of the cake. This way all of the ruffles will be uniform.

## STEP 4
When you reach the top of each ruffle, stop squeezing, and lift the tip away from the cake. If you leave a tail of frosting, take a damp paintbrush and smooth down the end of the frosting.

# Piping pearls

Piping pearls onto a cake really brings the design to life. This technique is used all of the time because it truly makes a statement.

## STEP 1

Secure the tip in your piping bag, then fill it with your chosen frosting (see page 74).

## STEP 2

Hold the tip close to the cake surface, where you want the pearl to be, and gently squeeze your piping bag. Once you are happy with the size of pearl you have formed, stop squeezing and gently pull away from the cake.

## STEP 3

After piping all of the pearls, use a dampened paintbrush to press the peak down gently on each pearl so it forms a perfectly round shape.

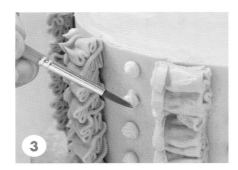

### USING THIS SKILL
Vertical Ruffles and Pearls Cake:
page 120

## EQUIPMENT

*Piping bag*

*Wilton No. 7 round decorating tip*

*Paintbrush*

### FURTHERING YOUR SKILLS

**This technique works well with both frosting and royal icing. If you use royal icing you can then dust with a pearlescent shimmer powder once the pearls have hardened.**

# Ruched piping

This technique is great to use if you are short on time and are looking to add texture to a design – perfect for cakes with multiple tiers.

**USING THIS SKILL**
Ruched Fabric Cake: page 124

### STEP 1
Secure the tip in your piping bag, then fill it with your chosen frosting (see page 74).

### STEP 2
Hold the piping bag so that the tip is parallel to the cake's surface.

### STEP 3
Pipe the frosting in a random pattern of ribbons. Move the tip from side to side and up and down, to create an organic shape. Keep the piping close together so that you cannot tell where the last section finished and the next one starts.

## EQUIPMENT

Piping bag

Wilton No. 104 petal decorating tip

Paintbrush

## FURTHERING YOUR SKILLS

A smooth consistency to your frosting will help you to pipe this design because you need the frosting to flow easily from the piping tip.

# Classic swirl cupcakes

This is often the first design that cake decorators learn. I will help you achieve the perfect swirl. In the beginning, you may prefer to create a swirl using just one colour frosting. As you get more comfortable, you will be able to swirl two colours together.

## SKILLS FOR REVIEW
Piping techniques: page 74
Piping a rose swirl: page 82

### EQUIPMENT

Wilton No. 2D drop flower decorating tip

Piping bags

### INGREDIENTS

12 cupcakes from the basic recipe (see page 23)

1 quantity frosting in the colour and flavour of your choice (see page 28)

Edible flowers, to decorate

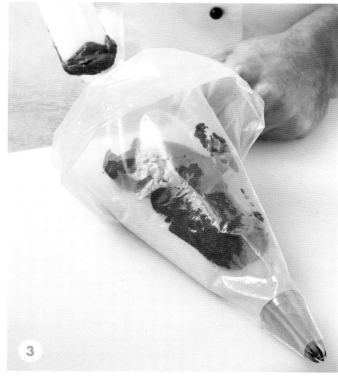

## STEP 1
Divide the frosting into two bowls. Colour one half with the colour of your choice (see page 29).

## STEP 2
Secure the tip in your piping bag. Fill it with plain frosting on one side.

## STEP 3
Fill the other side with coloured frosting. Gently squeeze the bag over a bowl until you see both the frosting colours emerge from the piping tip.

### STEP 4

Wipe off the tip. Now you are ready to pipe a swirl onto each cupcake. Starting with a central, single, squeeze of frosting. Continue piping to create a two-toned swirl that covers the surface of the cupcake.

### STEP 5

Decorate the top of the swirl with an edible flower.

### FURTHERING YOUR SKILLS

- You can use open star and drop flower decorating tips to pipe swirls onto the cupcakes. Experiment with different tips, to see which ones you prefer.

- An open star tip is ideal for beginners. The swirl it produces also stands up well in hot weather. The overall shape of it makes the swirl good to use in humidity as well.

# Simple swirl cupcakes

These cupcakes are so simple to make and look great in bright colours, muted tones and pastels alike.

**SKILLS FOR REVIEW**
Piping techniques: page 74
Piping a simple swirl: page 78

## EQUIPMENT

Wilton No. 2D drop flower piping tip

Piping bag

## INGREDIENTS

12 cupcakes from the basic recipe (see page 23)

1 quantity frosting in your chosen colour and flavour (see page 28)

Edible stars, to decorate

### STEP 1

Secure the tip in your piping bag, then fill it with your chosen frosting. Push the frosting into the tip of the bag and twist firmly to ensure you will have a good even pressure on the frosting as you pipe. This is important, as it will give a neat edge to the swirls.

### STEP 2

First pipe a small mound of frosting in the centre of the cupcake to look like a star and then move out in concentric circles, working to the edge of the cupcake. Once you have finished piping stop squeezing and lift the tip away.

### STEP 3

Finish the cake by decorating it with a sprinkling of edible stars.

### FURTHERING YOUR SKILLS

**Make this design more feminine by using small daisies to finish the cupcake.**

# Rose swirl cupcakes

This design may look like it took a while to do, but it seems more complicated than it is. With its intricate swirls and fine edges, this design has style. Follow my instructions and you will find this to be one of the simplest skills to learn.

### SKILLS FOR REVIEW

Flat topping a cupcake: page 66
Piping techniques: page 74
Piping a rose swirl: page 82

## EQUIPMENT

*Palette knife*

*Wilton No. 2D drop flower piping tip*

*Piping bag*

## INGREDIENTS

12 cupcakes from the basic recipe (see page 23)

1 quantity frosting in your chosen colour and flavour (see page 28)

Small edible leaves, to decorate

### FURTHERING YOUR SKILLS

- Practise this technique using a small version of this tip and pipe many small roses to create a bouquet effect.

- Keep your frosting colour realistic for the best results. Think of the natural colour of a rose.

## STEP 1
Using the palette knife, flat top each cupcake as described on page 66, but do not cover the frosting with a circle of fondant.

## STEP 2
Secure the tip in your piping bag and then fill it with your chosen frosting. Push the frosting into the tip of the bag and twist firmly, so you have an even pressure on the frosting as you pipe. It is important to do this to get neat edges on the petals.

## STEP 3
Starting at the centre of the cupcake, hold your piping bag vertically above the cupcake and make a rose swirl as described on page 82.

## STEP 4
To finish the design, take a small leaf and place it over the peak, at the end of your piping.

# Rosette cupcakes

From winning rosettes to vintage corsages, this frosting design lends itself to many different occasions.

## SKILLS FOR REVIEW
Flat topping a cupcake: page 66
Piping techniques: page 74
Piping a rosette: page 84

## EQUIPMENT

Metal heart cutter

Palette knife

PME FT070 piping tip

Piping bag

## INGREDIENTS

12 cupcakes from the basic recipe (see page 23)

1 quantity frosting in your chosen colour and flavour (see page 28)

Printed icing sheet, to decorate

### FURTHERING YOUR SKILLS

This design works very well with vibrant colours. Try layering two different colours to give the cupcake a whole new look.

### STEP 1

Cut a heart from the printed icing sheet using the heart cutter.

### STEP 2

Using the palette knife, flat top each cupcake as described on page 66, but do not cover the frosting with a circle of fondant.

### STEP 3

Secure the tip in your piping bag, then fill it with your chosen frosting.

### STEP 4

Holding the piping bag so the opening of the tip is horizontal to the cake and facing directly down, pipe a rosette on to each cupcake, as described on page 84.

### STEP 5

Take one of the hearts and place it on the centre of a cupcake to hide the space where all of the ruffles meet in the middle of the design.

# Snowflake cupcakes

This technique is known for its subtle elegance – less really is more with this design. This style of cupcake is often seen in high-end bakeries.

**SKILLS FOR REVIEW**
Flat topping a cupcake: page 66
Piping techniques: page 74

## EQUIPMENT

Snowflake cutter

Palette knife

Wilton No. 1A round decorating tip

Piping bag

## INGREDIENTS

12 cupcakes from the basic recipe (see page 23)

1 quantity frosting in your chosen colour and flavour (see page 28)

1 quantity gum paste (see page 36)

## STEP 1

Using the palette knife, flat top each cupcake as described on page 66, but do not cover the frosting with a circle of fondant.

## STEP 2

Instead, take the gum paste and roll it out until it is around 3 mm (⅛ in.) thick. Cut out a snowflake and allow it to dry on a flat surface for 30 minutes.

## STEP 3

Secure the tip in your piping bag and fill it with your chosen frosting.

## STEP 4

Hold the piping tip just above the surface of the cupcake (with the bag held vertically above the cupcake). Squeeze the bag firmly and pipe the frosting in a large circle onto the cupcake.

## STEP 5

Continue piping circles to cover the surface of each of the cupcakes.

## STEP 6

Add the snowflake to the centre of the cupcakes to finish.

### FURTHERING YOUR SKILLS

**Practise this design on a trial cupcake until you feel comfortable with the technique. Piping neat circles can be tricky and practise makes perfect.**

# Furry monster cupcakes

These furry monsters are great for a child's birthday and are so much fun to make. There are so many ways to decorate these. You will have hours of entertainment trying to come up with new ideas.

**SKILLS FOR REVIEW**
Flat topping a cupcake: page 66
Piping techniques: page 74
Creating a fur effect: page 90

## EQUIPMENT

*Palette knife*

*Piping bag*

*Wilton No. 233 multi-opening decorating tip*

## INGREDIENTS

12 cupcakes from the basic recipe (see page 23)

1 quantity frosting in your chosen colour and flavour (see page 28)

⅛ quantity gum paste in white (see page 36)

Edible food pen in black

**FURTHERING YOUR SKILLS**

- Try piping in two different colours to create a whole new breed of monster.

- Experiment with making arms and antennae to give your monsters different characteristics.

**STEP 1**

Using the palette knife, flat top each cupcake as described on page 66, but don't cover the frosting with a circle of fondant.

**STEP 2**

Secure the tip in your piping bag and fill it with your chosen frosting.

**STEP 3**

Holding the piping tip directly over each cupcake, squeeze out the frosting to create a fur effect.

**STEP 4**

To make each monster's eyes, roll two small balls of the gum paste and allow them to dry.

**STEP 5**

Draw on pupils using the edible food pen and add them to the monster's face.

# Grass effect cupcakes

This is the perfect cupcake for someone who loves to garden. In this recipe, I give you two ideas for ways to decorate them using piped grass.

**SKILLS FOR REVIEW**
Flat topping a cupcake: page 66
Piping techniques: page 74
Piping a grass effect: page 91

## EQUIPMENT

Palette knife

Wilton No. 233 multi-opening decorating tip

Piping bag

Small daisy plunger cutter

Cel former or drying foam

Fine paintbrush

## INGREDIENTS

12 cupcakes from the basic recipe (see page 23)

1 quantity frosting in green (see page 28)

1 quantity gum paste in gray, white and yellow (see page 36)

## FURTHERING YOUR SKILLS

- **Make small flowers in different colours.**

- **Experiment with making ladybirds to adorn your cupcakes.**

- **For a sports theme, replace the daisies with footballs, rugby balls or golf balls.**

### STEP 1
Using the palette knife, flat top each cupcake as described on page 66, but don't cover the frosting with a circle of fondant.

### STEP 2
Take the gray gum paste and roll out about 10 pea-sized balls. Flatten them with your fingertips and place them, as shown, to create a cobblestone path.

### STEP 3
For the flowers, roll out the white gum paste, cut out a few daisies for each cupcake, and place them on the cel former. Add a small ball of yellow paste to the centre of each daisy, using a damp paintbrush to help them stick and set aside to dry.

### STEP 4
Secure the tip in your piping bag, then fill it with your chosen frosting.

### STEP 5
Hold the tip vertically above the cake and squeeze out the frosting, to create a grass effect all over the plain areas on either side of the cobblestone path. Also decorate a few cupcakes just with the grass effect.

### STEP 6
Decorate each cupcake by adding one or two daisies next to the path or scattered across the grass.

# Rustic textured cake

The textured frosting on this cake is simple to master and looks amazing when coupled with a pretty, cheerful daisy.

**SKILLS FOR REVIEW**
Filling and crumb coating a cake:
page 50
Piping techniques: page 74
Texturising frosting: page 88

## EQUIPMENT

Palette knife

Large daisy plunger cutter

Cel former or drying foam

Fine paintbrush

## INGREDIENTS

13 cm (5 in.) round basic sponge cake
(see page 20)

18 cm (7 in.) round basic sponge cake
(see page 20)

1 quantity frosting in your chosen colour
and flavour (see page 28)

1 quantity gum paste in white
(see page 36)

Edible glue (see page 41)

Edible pearls, to decorate

### STEP 1
Using the frosting, fill and crumb coat each of the cakes as described on page 50 before stacking them on the cake board, on the turntable.

### STEP 2
Liberally spread frosting over both of the cakes, with a coating of about 3 cm (1 ¼ in.) all over. This will not stay this thick once you have created the textured pattern.

### STEP 3
Take the palette knife and, starting on the side of the base tier, make small curved strokes across the frosting. Clean your knife after each stroke on the side of a bowl.

Make the strokes in a random pattern to keep it organic and rustic looking. Sweep to the left, to the right, up and down, all over the cake.

### STEP 4
Work your way up the top tier of the cake using the same method as you did for the sides.

### STEP 5
Once your cake is textured you will need to make the flower. Take the gum paste and roll it out until it is around 3 mm (⅛ in.) thick. Press the daisy cutter into the paste and move it from left to right to cut through the paste. Press down the plunger and then lift away from the surface.

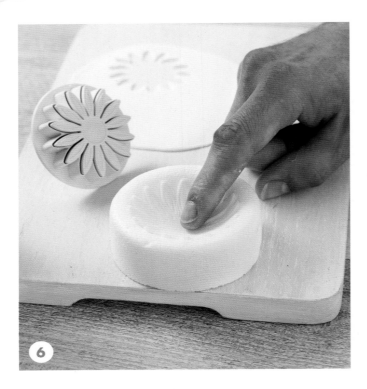

### STEP 6

Rest the daisy in the cel former and gently press the centre down to form a cup shape. Let it dry for 30 minutes.

### STEP 7

Roll out the gum paste again and cut another daisy. Place it in the cel former over the top of the previous daisy adding a small touch of edible glue, to help it adhere to the other daisy. Let the flower dry for another 30 minutes.

### STEP 8

To finish the daisy, add glue to the centre and stick on the pearls. Set aside to dry, then position the daisy on the bottom layer of the cake to finish.

### FURTHERING YOUR SKILLS

This cake would look wonderful with cascading leaves down one side instead of the daisies. It would give it a lovely autumnal style.

# Layered cake

Here is a beautiful cake, piped with layers of ruffles, adorned with beautiful ribbon roses and leaves.

**SKILLS FOR REVIEW**
Filling and crumb coating a cake: page 50
Piping techniques: page 74
Piping horizontal ruffles: page 92
Making a ribbon rose: page 209

## EQUIPMENT

*Wilton No. 127 petal decorating tip*　　*Piping bag*

*Fine paintbrush*　　*Leaf cutter*

## INGREDIENTS

18 cm (7 in.) round basic sponge cake (see page 20)

1 quantity frosting in your chosen colour and flavour (see page 28)

1 quantity gum paste in yellow and green (see page 36)

## STEP 1
Fill and crumb coat the cake as described on page 50.

## STEP 2
Secure the tip in your piping bag and fill it with your chosen frosting. Work from the top of the cake to the bottom, piping horizontal ruffles.

## STEP 3
Once finished, use a damp paintbrush to wipe away any excess frosting from the stand.

## STEP 4
Make three ribbon roses from the yellow gum paste and set them aside to dry for about 30 minutes.

## STEP 5
To make the leaves, roll out the green gum paste until it is about 3 mm (¹⁄₈ in.) thick and cut out the shapes using the leaf cutter. Set them aside to dry for about 30 minutes.

## STEP 6
Add the flowers and leaves to the side of the cake. If the frosting has crusted, you may want to add a small amount of fresh frosting to the back of each flower before gently pressing them into the frosting.

### FURTHERING YOUR SKILLS

- To create a fun Easter design, decorate this cake with small ovals cut from patterned edible paper.

- This cake also works well coated in chocolate frosting and finished off with roses made from modelling chocolate (see page 138).

# Vertical ruffles and pearls cake

This simply beautiful design looks just as stunning on cupcakes. The pearls are a perfect complement to the elegant ruffles. The vintage look of this cake would be delightful for a tea party.

**SKILLS FOR REVIEW**
Piping techniques: page 74
Piping vertical ruffles: page 94
Piping pearls: page 96

## EQUIPMENT

Turntable

Palette knife

PME FT070 piping tip

Wilton No. 7 round decorating tip

Piping bag

Metal scraper

Fine paintbrush

## INGREDIENTS

18 cm (7 in.) round basic sponge cake (see page 20)

1 quantity frosting in your chosen colour and flavour (see page 28)

### STEP 1
Fill and crumb coat the cake as described on page 50.

### STEP 2
Spoon a large amount of frosting onto the top of the cake and spread it evenly across the surface. Hold the palette knife halfway across the cake, parallel with the top but slightly tilted. Slowly turn the turntable so that the frosting is gently flattened beneath the palette knife. You will be left with a small dot in the centre of the cake. Use the palette knife to gently blend the surface of the frosting.

### STEP 3
Continuing to use the palette knife while slowly spinning the turntable, spread more frosting around the sides of the cake, using the knife vertically and sweeping from side to side.

### STEP 4
Using the metal scraper, with the bottom edge flat on the base board or turntable, and the side straight against the edge of the cake, turn the turntable continuously until you have a smooth vertical side to the cake. If the cake is not flat yet, wipe away the excess from the scraper and repeat until the frosting is smooth.

### STEP 5

Remove any excess frosting from the top edge, using inward sweeping motions of the palette knife. As in Step 2, hold the spatula at an angle as you do this. Continue until the top of the cake is smooth.

### STEP 6

Chill the cake in the fridge for 30 minutes. This will help the frosting form a light crust so it is easier to pipe on.

### STEP 7

Secure the FT070 tip in your piping bag, then fill it with your chosen frosting.

### STEP 8

Hold the piping tip with the opening horizontally facing the side of the cake, and pipe vertical ruffles 6 cm (2 ¼ in.) apart until the side of the cake is covered.

## STEP 9

Once you have piped all the ruffles, change the piping tip to the Wilton No. 7 tip. Hold the tip close to the bottom of the cake, between two of the ruffles, and gently squeeze the piping bag to form a pearl shape. When you are happy with the size, stop squeezing and gently pull away from the cake. Repeat this step between each ruffle around the cake.

## STEP 10

After piping all of the pearls, use a dampened paintbrush to gently press down the peak on each pearl, so it forms a perfectly round shape.

### FURTHERING YOUR SKILLS

- Turn the cake slowly to create a dense ruffle or fast for small, loose ruffles.

- Pipe two rows of pearls between each ruffle to make this cake even more special.

# Ruched fabric cake

This cake is covered in what looks like an endless ribbon of frosting. Its vintage appearance is extremely popular. The wavy texture gives this cake simple elegance.

**SKILLS FOR REVIEW**
Filling and crumb coating a cake: page 50
Piping techniques: page 74
Ruched piping: page 97

## EQUIPMENT

*23 cm (9 in.) diameter round cake board*

*Wilton No. 104 petal decorating tip*

*Piping bag*

## INGREDIENTS

18 cm (7 in.) round basic sponge cake (see page 20)

1 quantity frosting in your chosen colour and flavour (see page 28)

## STEP 1

Fill and crumb coat the cake as described on page 50.

## STEP 2

Secure the tip in your piping bag and fill it with your chosen frosting.

## STEP 3

Hold your piping bag so that the wider opening of the piping tip is closest to the cake, and pipe the frosting in a random pattern of ruched fabric.

## STEP 4

Once you have piped the sides, move up and onto the top of the cake. Make sure that every part of the cake is covered.

### FURTHERING YOUR SKILLS

- This design is great for the top tier of a layered cake. It adds depth and variation to the cake.

- This design would look particularly good if you piped it in rainbow colours.

# Working with chocolate

Is there anyone who does not like chocolate? You would be surprised at just how many things you can do with this wonderful edible medium. From filling a cake, to covering it, and making decorations, it is so versatile. It is incredibly sophisticated as a cake covering.

# Melting candy melts

Candy melts give cake pops or cakes a velvety chocolate coating. Strictly speaking, they are not a chocolate product, but they are used in the same way as chocolate. I also feature them in one of my cake pop recipes in this chapter. They are designed to be simply melted in the microwave. They are a real timesaver because you do not have to temper them.

### STEP 1
Put the candy melts into a microwaveable container and put it into the microwave on high for 15 seconds. Stir the melts, then put them back in for 10 seconds and stir again. Put them back in the microwave for 10 second intervals, until you can see the candy melts are melted.

### STEP 2
When they are almost fully melted and you can see only tiny pieces remaining, mix them well until those lumps are melted. It will take about a minute until they are fully incorporated. You should then have a smooth, runny consistency.

### EQUIPMENT
Microwaveable container

### INGREDIENTS
Bag of candy melts

# Melting chocolate

There are two ways to melt chocolate – in a traditional bain marie or in the microwave. It can be all too easy to burn the chocolate in a microwave when melting it, so although both methods are given here, it is generally safer to use a bain marie.

### STEP 1
Choose a heatproof bowl that sits comfortably in the saucepan and does not touch the water.

### STEP 2
Pour enough water into the saucepan to cover its bottom by about 2.5 cm (1 in.). Bring the water to the boil then remove it from the heat.

### STEP 3
Put the chocolate in the bowl and rest it over the hot water to melt, removing from the heat to stir occasionally.

## EQUIPMENT

Heatproof bowl

## INGREDIENTS

Saucepan

### FURTHERING YOUR SKILLS

- To melt the chocolate in the microwave, place it in a microwaveable container and heat on high for 15 seconds, stir and repeat until melted. As the chocolate becomes warmer, reduce the time that you put it in the microwave for.

# Tempering chocolate

This process is important for helping chocolate keep its snap. It also gives the chocolate a shiny surface. There are several methods of tempering chocolate, but I find this one the easiest.

### STEP 1
Add two-thirds of the chocolate to the bowl. Place the bowl over a saucepan of barely-simmering water, and make sure that the bowl is not touching the water. Allow the chocolate to melt slowly.

### STEP 2
Once melted, add the remaining chocolate, stir and test the temperature.

### STEP 3
Continue to stir until the chocolate reaches 31–32°C (88–90°F) for dark chocolate, 30–31°C (86–88°F) for milk chocolate and 27–28°C (80–82°F) for white chocolate.

## EQUIPMENT

Heatproof bowl

Flexible spatula

Thermometer

## INGREDIENTS

Milk, dark or white chocolate, broken into even pieces

## FURTHERING YOUR SKILLS

- If you are short on time, chocolate can be tempered in the microwave. Heat two-thirds of the chocolate in a microwaveable bowl on high for 15 seconds, stir and repeat until melted, then add the remainder and stir, without heating, until all of the chocolate has melted. Do not use a glass bowl when melting chocolate in the microwave because it retains its heat.

- Use Belgian chocolate with a minimum of 30 per cent cocoa butter. That is how you get a quality taste and a nice finish to your chocolate.

# Making chocolate panels

Chocolate panels are an ideal way to cover a cake. You can really punch up the design by putting a transfer sheet pattern on it. I will show you how to make enough panels to cover a 15 cm (6 in.) square cake.

**USING THIS SKILL**
Chocolate Panel Cake: page 148

## EQUIPMENT

3 transfer sheets

Craft knife

Spatula

Wax paper

Ruler

## INGREDIENTS

400 g (14 oz.) milk, dark or white chocolate

### STEP 1
Cut the transfer sheets into rectangles measuring 10 x 30 cm (4 x 12 in.). Use the craft knife and a ruler to ensure the edges remain neat.

### STEP 2
Place three of the transfer rectangles on the work surface at a time. Put the sheet shiny-side down. This is the side with the design that you will want the chocolate to touch.

### STEP 3
Pour a small amount of tempered chocolate (see page 130) over the transfer rectangles, one at a time, and spread out to a thin coating using a spatula.

### STEP 4
Move the strips to one side before they set, and remove the excess chocolate from the work area.

## STEP 5

As the rectangles start to set, you will notice they become duller and firmer in appearance. This is the perfect time to cut the chocolate into strips. Line up the ruler with the longest edge of the strip and mark every 5 cm (2 in.) with the craft knife.

## STEP 6

Turn the ruler and score into 5 cm (2 in.) wide strips using the markers as a guideline.

## STEP 7

At this point, you will want to chill the panels. If you do not do this, the chocolate can shrink and twist. Place a piece of wax paper across the transfer strips, then place a lightweight baking tray over the wax paper. The light tray will be enough weight to prevent the panels from changing shape. Place them in the fridge for 8–10 minutes.

## STEP 8

Once set, peel away the wax paper and carefully remove the transfer sheet leaving the printed pattern on the chocolate. When you remove the transfer strips from the chocolate, do one as a test strip first. If you find the pattern doesn't come away with the chocolate, leave the strips to set for a short while longer. Once the transfers are removed, the panels will break into the rectangles where you have scored it, then you are ready to put it on your cakes.

8

# Making chocolate fans

Chocolate fans look great as a cake topping or as a side decoration. Once you have mastered this technique, you are going to want to add them to every cake you make. Although you can use dark, milk or white chocolate to make the fans, milk chocolate is the easiest to work with.

**USING THIS SKILL**
Two-tier Centrepiece Cake: page 152

**EQUIPMENT**

*Marble cutting board*

*Palette knife*

*Craft knife*

**INGREDIENTS**

*400 g (14 oz.) milk, dark or white chocolate, for 9 fans*

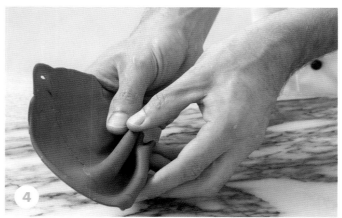

## STEP 1

Put the marble cutting board into the freezer for
2–3 hours.

## STEP 2

When you are ready to make the fans, temper the
chocolate (see page 130) and remove the marble cutting
board from the freezer. Spread a tablespoon of the
chocolate across the marble slab with the palette knife
into a rectangular shape.

## STEP 3

Use the craft knife to cut off each end of the chocolate
rectangle and then cut a line along the length of the
rectangle in the middle. You will have two strips, each
with a rough and straight edge.

## STEP 4

Working quickly before the chocolate sets, lift one of
the strips from the marble with your fingertips along the
rough edge and start to fan it out. Take the base of the
fan and squeeze it gently to make it stick together. Set
it aside and repeat with the next chocolate strip. Repeat
steps 2–4 until you have made enough fans or until you
have no more chocolate.

### FURTHERING YOUR SKILLS

If the marble board gets too warm as you make
the fans, place it back into the freezer for
30 minutes. Gently reheat the chocolate in a
bowl over a pot of boiling water or in the
microwave so you can work with it again.

# Making chocolate roses

What could be more appetising than chocolate that looks like a rose? You will be hooked once you start making these. You will need a small quantity of modelling chocolate for each rose (see page 30).

**USING THIS SKILL**
Chocolate Romance Cake: page 150

## EQUIPMENT

*Single petal cutter*

*Palette knife*

## INGREDIENTS

*1 quantity modelling chocolate (see page 30)*

### STEP 1

Take a small ball of modelling chocolate and mould it into a cone shape. Put it onto your work surface. It is going to be the centre of your flower.

### STEP 2

Roll out the chocolate and cut out three petals with the petal cutter. Wrap the rest of the chocolate in cling film to keep it moist and fresh.

### STEP 3

Starting with one petal, wrap it around the cone until the petal curls around. This will form your bud.

### STEP 4

Take the next two petals and attach them on opposite sides. Curl back the edges and pinch the petal in the centre of the edge.

### STEP 5

Now roll out your chocolate again and cut out three more petals. Store the chocolate once again. Take the three petals and stagger them one-by-one at staggered points around the rose. As before, curl back the edges using your fingertips and pinch the centre edge.

## STEP 8

Use the palette knife to slice the rose away from the cone. This will give it a flat back for you to attach to your cake.

## STEP 6

Roll out the remaining chocolate and cut out five further petals. Again, stagger them around the rose. Repeat by curling back the edges and pinching the petals of the rose.

## STEP 7

Your rose is now finished. If you want a bigger rose, repeat Step 6 until you are happy with the size of your flower.

### FURTHERING YOUR SKILLS

Dust your finished rose with lustre dust for a luxurious appearance.

# Making chocolate buttons

Chocolate buttons are really easy to make. I will show you how to make them with a pretty pattern on one side, using a chocolate transfer sheet.

**USING THIS SKILL**
Two-tier Centrepiece Cake: page 152

## EQUIPMENT

*2 transfer sheets*

*Piping bag*

*Small palette knife*

## INGREDIENTS

*400 g (14 oz.) milk, dark or white chocolate chips, for 32 buttons*

**FURTHERING YOUR SKILLS**

- Do not throw away the used transfer sheet. You can make more buttons and put them on the areas of the sheet that still have the pattern left.

- Remember that you can make them as big or as small as you want.

**STEP 1**

Temper the chocolate (see page 130).

**STEP 2**

Lay the chocolate transfer sheet, shiny-side down, on a work surface. Ensure the dull side of the sheet rather than the glossy side is facing up, as this is the side with the transfer on it. This is the side that you want the chocolate to come into contact with.

**STEP 3**

Fill the piping bag with some of the tempered chocolate. Snip off the very tip of the piping bag and begin to pipe small circles on the transfer sheet.

**STEP 4**

If you are having trouble levelling out the chocolate, use a small palette knife to help you out.

**STEP 5**

Let the chocolate buttons sit for about 30 minutes. Then carefully peel the transfer sheet away from the chocolate buttons. The pattern will remain on the surface, but if you find the pattern doesn't come off with the chocolate, let the buttons set for a little longer.

# Rose cake pops

These roses are just as nice a surprise as getting a bouquet of real roses – perfectly delicious and romantic too. For a truly original centrepiece, display them in a tall vase to look like flowers. They are also an ideal gift and party favour.

**SKILLS FOR REVIEW**
Melting candy melts: page 128
Piping techniques: page 74

## EQUIPMENT

*Styrofoam*

*Piping bag*

*Green ribbon, to decorate (optional)*

## INGREDIENTS

*24 cake pops (see page 26)*

*400 g (14 oz.) red candy melts*

*150 g (5 oz.) red sanding sugar*

### STEP 1

To cover the cake pops, melt the candy melts and gently dip each pop into it. As you remove the pop, turn it to catch any drips, for a smooth finish. Stand the cake pops in the styrofoam to dry and set aside the remaining melted candy.

### STEP 2

Once the chocolate on the cake pops has hardened, melt the remaining candy melts once again in the microwave, in 8 second intervals, until the mixture is smooth again.

### STEP 3

Pour the candy melts into the piping bag and twist the top to get it ready to pipe. Snip off the very tip to reveal a tiny hole at the end.

### STEP 4

Hold the cake pop in one hand while you pipe with the other. Gently squeeze the piping bag and pipe a spiral on the top of the cake pop.

### STEP 5

Use a teaspoon to sprinkle the red sanding sugar over the top. Return each decorated cake pop to the styrofoam and let it harden. The sugar makes the top of the rose glisten.

### STEP 6

Finish off the stick of each rose cake pop with a bow made from green ribbon, if you would like.

### FURTHERING YOUR SKILLS

**To add a little more sparkle, add edible glitter. It will look great with the red sanding sugar.**

# Chocolate drizzle cake pops

Cake pops are a great alternative to cakes and cupcakes. They are very popular and make great gifts and party favours. These chocolaty drizzled cake pops are easy to decorate and are ideal for any occasion.

**SKILLS FOR REVIEW**
Tempering chocolate: page 130
Melting chocolate: page 129

## EQUIPMENT

*Styrofoam*

*Piping bag*

## INGREDIENTS

*24 cake pops (see page 26)*

*680 g (1 ½ lbs.) milk chocolate, broken into pieces*

*200 g (7 oz.) white chocolate, broken into pieces*

### STEP 3

Hold a cake pop in one hand while you pipe with the other. Gently squeeze the piping bag and turn the cake pop slowly so you get smooth lines. Once you have enough coating, return each pop to the styrofoam to harden.

### STEP 4

Now they are ready to eat. Also, you can package them in small plastic wrappers and give them out to people. You can buy the wrappers in most cake supply shops.

### STEP 1

To cover the cake pops, temper the milk chocolate and gently dip each pop into it. As you remove the pop, turn it to catch any drips for a smooth finish. Stand the cake pops in the styrofoam to harden.

### STEP 2

For the decoration, melt the white chocolate. Pour it into the piping bag and twist the top to get it ready to pipe. Snip off the tip to reveal a tiny hole at the end.

---

#### FURTHERING YOUR SKILLS

**When you are piping, keep a small plate under the cake pop to avoid making a mess.**

---

# Chocolate panel cake

Of all my cakes, this particular one is my favourite to give as a gift. It is super easy to make and its rich flavour makes it the perfect dessert. Once you make it for somebody, they will request it time and time again.

**SKILLS FOR REVIEW**
Making chocolate panels: page 132
Filling and crumb coating a cake: page 50
Piping a rose swirl: page 82

### EQUIPMENT

*Wilton No. 2D drop flower decorating tip*

*Piping bag*

### INGREDIENTS

*18 cm (7 in.) basic sponge cake, cooked in a 15 cm (6 in.) x 8 cm (3 in.) tall square tin (see page 20)*

*2 quantities white chocolate frosting (see page 28)*

*Chocolate panels that are 5 cm (2 in.) wide and made from 3 transfer sheets (see page 132)*

### STEP 1

Using the white chocolate frosting, fill and crumb coat the cake to get it ready to fix the panels into place. You will need a thicker crumb coat than usual because you are going to stick the panels to this layer.

### STEP 2

Position the chocolate panels on the side of the cake, overlapping each panel slightly as you add them – they should stick to the frosting very easily. Work around the cake until all of the sides are covered.

### STEP 3

Secure the drop flower decorating tip in your piping bag, then fill it with the remaining white chocolate frosting. Pipe rose swirls across the top of the cake.

### STEP 4

Using the same piping tip, fill in the gaps with small piped stars of frosting. Squeeze the piping bag, then release to create a single piece of frosting that looks like a star.

# Chocolate romance cake

The perfect combination of romantic and sumptuous, this cake is absolutely heavenly. The rich chocolate frosting coupled with the chocolate roses and rolled wafers will make you a chocolate lover, if you aren't already.

## SKILLS FOR REVIEW
Making chocolate roses: page 138
Filling and crumb coating a cake: page 50

### EQUIPMENT

*Palette knife*

### INGREDIENTS

*18 cm (7 in.) round basic sponge cake (see page 20)*

*1 quantity chocolate frosting (see page 28)*

*500 g (1 lb. 2 oz.) shop-bought plain, milk or white chocolate rolled wafers, or a mixture of each*

*15 chocolate roses (see page 138)*

**5**

## FURTHERING YOUR SKILLS

Decorate the top of this cake with fresh fruit, such as raspberries or blueberries, instead of the modelled roses – it will look sensational.

**STEP 1**
Make 15 chocolate roses and set them aside.

**STEP 2**
Using the chocolate frosting, fill and crumb coat the cake.

**STEP 3**
Take the rolled wafers and decide how you want to put them around the cake. Start by laying them out along your work surface how you want them to look.

**STEP 4**
Place the rolled wafers around the edge of the cake one at a time, until the whole cake is surrounded in them.

**STEP 5**
To finish, cover the top of the cake with chocolate roses.

# Two-tier centrepiece cake

Covered with chocolate fondant and decorated with handmade chocolate buttons and fans, this cake is a real showstopper. It will have all your guests talking.

## SKILLS FOR REVIEW
Filling and crumb coating a cake:
page 50
Dowelling a cake: page 62
Making chocolate buttons: page 142
Making chocolate fans: page 136

### EQUIPMENT

Marble cutting board

Jumbo straws

Piping bag

### INGREDIENTS

13 cm (5 in.) round basic sponge cake (see page 20)

18 cm (7 in.) round basic sponge cake (see page 20)

1 quantity chocolate frosting (see page 28)

2 kg (4 lbs. 8 oz.) shop-bought chocolate fondant

500 g (1 lb. 2 oz.) milk chocolate, tempered (see page 130)

### STEP 1

Using one-third of the chocolate frosting, fill and crumb coat each of the cakes. Do not stack them yet.

### STEP 2

Cover both cakes individually with the chocolate fondant. Set aside to dry and place your marble cutting board in the freezer, ready for making the chocolate fans.

### STEP 3

Dowel the cakes together using the remaining frosting.

### STEP 4

Make about 32 chocolate buttons to cover the base of each cake. Set them aside for about 30 minutes to dry.

### STEP 5

Meanwhile, remove the marble cutting board from the freezer and make 9 chocolate fans for the top of the cake.

### STEP 6

Carefully remove the chocolate buttons from the transfer sheet. Use a little of the remaining tempered chocolate to attach them, in a single line, around the base of each cake. Be sure to attach them with the pattern side facing outwards.

### STEP 7

Finally, use a small amount of the tempered chocolate to attach the fans to the top of the cake.

153

# Working with fondant

Fondant is a particularly popular cake covering because it is so adaptable. It is a sweet, pliable frosting that can be rolled flat for covering cakes, and it sets firm over time. See pages 34 and 35 for a basic fondant recipe and how to colour it.

# Using foam drying balls

A foam drying ball allows you to create domes of fondant for covering cupcakes. This is my favourite technique because it lets you achieve really professional looking results with minimum stress.

**USING THIS SKILL**
Tennis Ball Cupcakes: page 200

### EQUIPMENT

*Foam drying ball*

*8 cm (3 ¼ in.) or 7 cm (2 ¾ in.) diameter circle cutter*

## STEP 1

Roll out a walnut-sized piece of fondant and cut out a circle using either of the cutters, depending on the size of your cupcake. For the cupcake recipes in this book, I suggest that you use the larger size of cutter.

## STEP 2

Carefully place the fondant circle over the foam drying ball.

## STEP 3

Smooth the fondant circle down at the edges so that it becomes a dome. Set it aside for about 40 minutes until the fondant has dried and can be easily lifted off the dome without losing its shape.

## STEP 4

To cover the cupcake, top the cupcake with frosting, turn the dried fondant dome over and lightly press it in place.

### FURTHERING YOUR SKILLS

If you are in a hurry, or you want to ensure your domes dry particularly solid, use gum paste in place of fondant (see page 206).

# Embossing fondant

*You don't have to stop at plain flat cake surfaces anymore. You can now emboss a whole range of patterns into the fondant.*

### STEP 1

Make sure the fondant is warm and pliable and then roll it out until the fondant is a little thicker than usual for covering a cake or cupcake. This is because when you press the embossing folder onto the fondant, you will thin it out more.

### STEP 2

Take the embossing folder and hold it against the fondant with one hand. Use your other hand to press it down firmly across the fondant. Lift the folder away from the fondant to reveal the pattern.

### STEP 3

Without squashing the design, carefully apply your fondant to flat topped cupcakes.

2

3

## EQUIPMENT

*Embossing folder*

## FURTHERING YOUR SKILLS

You will find embossing folders in the card-making section of craft shops, and they work perfectly for cupcakes. They are less expensive than specialist cake embossing sheets, and card-making embossing folders come in a much wider variety of patterns.

# Using the scriber tool

The scriber tool is one of the most useful fondant modelling tools that you can buy. There is a narrow end and a wider end, both of which have their own particular uses.

1

### STEP 1
The narrow end is good for adding delicate details such as drawing veins on leaves and flowers, or drawing texturing marks on fondant.

### STEP 2
The wider end is best used for larger indentations, or if you're making petals, adding wider veins and fluting. I also find this tool particularly useful for making toes and fingers on models – or for styling hair.

# Cutting fondant strips

Fondant strips can be tricky, but this method makes it as straightforward as possible.

### STEP 1
Roll out the fondant to your required thickness (see page 54) and then push the cutter along the fondant.

### STEP 2
Make sure you cut each strip using only one roll of the cutter, as this will keep you from distorting the shape of the fondant while you cut.

### STEP 3
If you are attaching the strips vertically on a cake, it is best to give them 15 minutes to firm up slightly before moving them so that they keep their shape.

## EQUIPMENT

*Multi ribbon cutter*

## FURTHERING YOUR SKILLS

If you find your fondant is too soft, knead in 1 teaspoon of CMC powder for each 250 g (9 oz.) of fondant to make it firmer and easier to work with.

# Texturising fondant

Fondant is very adaptable, and you can add texture easily with either professional tools or common household objects. Prepare your texturising implements ahead of time before shaping or rolling out the fondant.

## STEP 1
Prepare the fondant as necessary – if rolling out, see page 54.

## STEP 2
Press the texturiser onto the fondant, or the fondant onto the texturizer, whichever works best in the circumstances. For example, to create a leather-like texture, scrunch up a piece of aluminium foil and blot it all over the fondant. Experiment with how much you scrunch up the foil for different finishes. You can also try a cheese grater, a sieve or the scriber tool to create a wood effect.

### FURTHERING YOUR SKILLS

Other items you can use are:

- A sieve to make grass

- A scriber tool to create a wood effect

- The zester area on a cheese grater to give an orange peel texture

### EQUIPMENT

*Texturiser of your choice*

# Using an extruder gun

This tool is incredibly versatile. It is supplied with many different nozzles that you can use to create all manner of decorations, from hair to rope (see Furthering your skills, page 163).

**SKILLS FOR REVIEW**
Mr Fluffles Cake: page 170
Tennis Ball Cupcakes: page 200

**EQUIPMENT**

*Extruder gun*

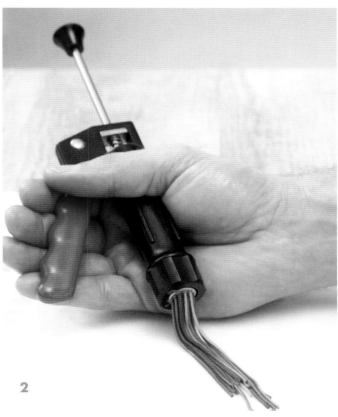

## STEP 1

Knead the fondant until it is really warm and soft. This will give it a gum-like texture and help it to push through the tiny holes in the extruder nozzle. Fill the extruder gun with the fondant.

## STEP 2

Squeeze the handle to push the fondant through the nozzle. You will need to use these decorations quickly to ensure the fondant does not dry out and become too fragile to work with.

### FURTHERING YOUR SKILLS

- Try using the extruder nozzle with the clover-shaped disc to create a rope effect. Squeeze the fondant in long lengths and then twist each end in opposite directions.

- The multiple opening nozzles work very well for making hair as you can achieve many different textures and styles (see page 170).

# Painting on fondant

This is a very popular technique and is a lot easier than it looks. Once you have mastered the skill, you can turn even the simplest of cakes into real works of art.

## EQUIPMENT

*Food colourings of your choice*

*Fine paintbrush*

*Clear alcohol or dipping solution*

*Paint palette*

### STEP 1
Before you paint on fondant, it must be completely dry. Otherwise, the paint will bleed into your fondant as you apply it.

### STEP 2
If you are using food colouring pastes or food colouring dusts, mix together a couple of drops of clear alcohol or dipping solution with $\frac{1}{2}$ teaspoon of the paste or powder on a paint palette to create a paint consistency.

### STEP 3
To start painting, dampen the paintbrush and use only the smallest amount of paint to ensure you don't apply too much colour.

### STEP 4
When you need to highlight areas in lighter colours, it is important to leave the first layer of paint to dry before moving onto the lighter colour. Otherwise, the colours will likely bleed into each other and ruin your design.

### FURTHERING YOUR SKILLS

- If you are unsure about how to paint a design, it's a good idea to roll out a spare piece of fondant, allow it to dry and use it for practise before moving onto the cake itself.

- Painting on a cake uses the same techniques as painting on paper and canvas, so research painting techniques to help you build your own designs and ideas.

# Shading on fondant

Sometimes you need to add just a little hint of colour to bring a design to life. For example, on the Monkey Cupcakes (see page 188), I found that adding a hint of pink shimmer powder to the cheeks made all the difference to the finished design.

### STEP 1
Put about ½ teaspoon of the colouring onto your paint palette.

### STEP 2
Load the paintbrush with a small amount of colouring – for shading, a dry powder will suffice – and then blot it on kitchen roll to remove the excess powder.

### STEP 3
Gently start to build up the colouring on the surface of the fondant.

### EQUIPMENT

Powdered food colourings of your choice

Paint palette

Fine paintbrush

### FURTHERING YOUR SKILLS

If you find you have added too much colour, you can tone it down by dusting over with corn flour.

# Slice of cake

This fun, creative, sculpted cake will excite your guests when they realise that it's not just a slice of cake, but a whole cake in itself.

## SKILLS FOR REVIEW
Filling and crumb coating a cake: page 50
Rolling out fondant: page 54
Painting on fondant: page 164

## EQUIPMENT

Craft knife

PME set of 3 heart plunger cutters

4 cm (1 ³⁄₄ in.) wide heart cutter

2 fine paintbrushes, for gluing and painting

Palette knife

## INGREDIENTS

18 cm (7 in.) round Madeira cake (see page 24)

1 quantity frosting in your chosen colour and flavour (see page 28)

1 quantity fondant in pale yellow, white, purple, pale green, blue and lilac (see page 34)

1 quantity fondant in pink (see page 34)

Edible glue (see page 41)

Food colouring paste in white

### STEP 1

To shape the cake, looking from above, mark a point at the edge of the cake and cut a line at approximately 30 degrees starting at this point to the left and the right, so that you end up with as large a piece from the cake as possible that looks like a giant slice of cake. Use the off-cuts to make cake pops (see page 26). As this design is made from a Madeira cake, there is no need to slice and fill it, but crumb coat it and chill for 30 minutes.

### STEP 2

Coat the cake in a second layer of crumb coat, and then roll out the pale yellow fondant and cover the cake. Trim the excess fondant and set aside – you will use this later.

### STEP 3

To make the top and side of the cake, roll out the remaining pink fondant and lay it across the outer edge and top of the cake. Use the craft knife to slice the fondant carefully so that it only covers the top and side of the slice. Once you have cut off the excess, use your fingertip to smooth the edge of the fondant and remove the square edge.

### STEP 4

Roll out a thin strip of white fondant. It needs to look quite lumpy as it is the thin strip of cream squirting out of the cake. Stick this in place halfway up the cake on each side of the wedge with a little edible glue. Do the same with a

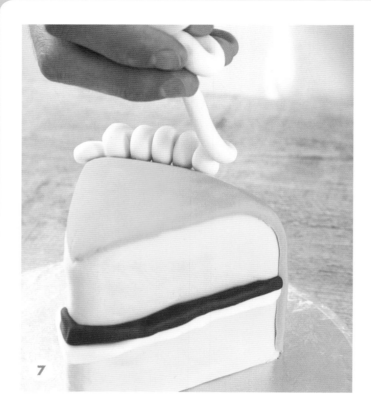

7

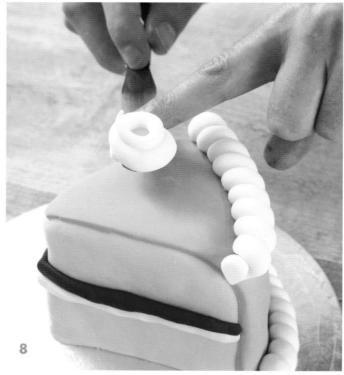

8

strip of rolled-out red fondant (to look like jam), sticking it directly above the white stripe.

## STEP 5
Roll out small pieces of pale green, pink and lilac fondants until they are about 3 mm (⅛ in.) thick. Use the plunger cutters to cut out hearts in all three sizes and leave them to dry on a flat surface.

## STEP 6
Roll out another walnut-sized piece of lilac fondant until it is about 3 mm (⅛ in.) thick. Cut out a large heart shape and leave to one side to dry.

## STEP 7
Roll out a long rounded strip of white fondant. Paint a thick line of glue along the top outer edge of the cake slice and then carefully glue the strip in place, turning the fondant in a spiral as you press it in place. Repeat this step at the outer base edge of the cake slice too.

## STEP 8
Take the small hearts, and using edible glue and one of the paintbrushes, attach the hearts to the two white spirals you have just made. Mix the colours and sizes well.

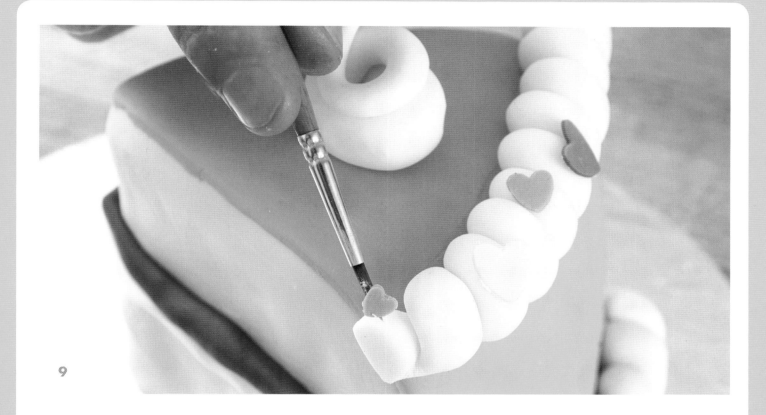

9

## STEP 9

Roll a small rounded strip of the white fondant and mould it into a small spiral so that is looks like whipped cream. Once you are happy with the shape, glue it in place on the top of the cake.

## STEP 10

Glue a heart on top of the fondant cream swirl. Then glue the other hearts along the bottom line of cream on the base of the cake.

### FURTHERING YOUR SKILLS

- To make a more boy-orientated cake, use bright colours and stars instead of the hearts – it's up to you.

- You can vary the size of the slice of cake depending on how many servings are needed.

# Mr Fluffles cake

Here is a furry fun monster cake that is sure to put a smile on everyone's face. The wonderfully colourful layers are made using an extruder gun (see page 162).

**SKILLS FOR REVIEW**
Filling and crumb coating a cake: page 50
Rolling out fondant: page 54
Using the scriber tool: page 159
Using an extruder gun: page 162

## EQUIPMENT

Scriber tool

4 cocktail sticks

Extruder gun

Paint palette

2 fine paintbrushes, for gluing and painting

## INGREDIENTS

18 cm (7 in.) round basic sponge cake (see page 20)

1 quantity frosting in your chosen colour and flavour (see page 28)

1 quantity gum paste in white (see page 36)

½ quantity fondant each in yellow, blue, orange, green and red (see page 34)

Edible glue (see page 41)

Food colouring powder in black

Clear alcohol or dipping solution

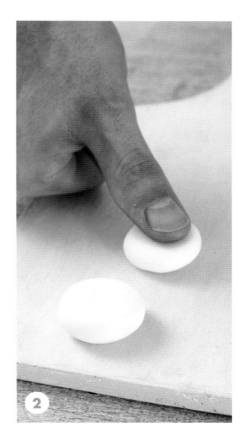

### STEP 1
Using the frosting, fill and crumb coat the cake. Cover the cake in white fondant.

### STEP 2
To make Mr Fluffles' hands, take two walnut-sized balls from the white gum paste, and use your thumb or finger to flatten them so you have a large round shape.

### STEP 3
Gently squeeze the base of the circle to make a wrist. Use the sharp end of your scriber tool to cut through the hand, once at a 45-degree angle for the thumb, then to make three vertical lines between each finger.

### STEP 4
Separate the fingers one at a time and gently roll them to round the fingers and give them a realistic shape.

### STEP 5
Shape the hands by moving the fingers to your desired pose. Try waving, giving the thumbs up, or maybe thumbs down. He will really come to life with hand gestures.

### STEP 6
Once you have decided on the pose, insert a cocktail stick through the centre of each hand and into the middle finger to give stability. Put the hands aside to dry and firm up a little.

### STEP 7

Insert the largest multiple-hole disc in the extruder gun and then fill it with the coloured fondant to go around the base of the cake. Begin to squeeze lengths of hair that are about 2.5 cm (1 in.) long. As the fondant emerges from the gun, it may be longer on one side than the other. Don't worry, this will give it life and make the hair look realistic.

### STEP 8

Attach each length of the hair as you detach it from the gun. Sweep your finger across the end of the gun to get it all off in one go and then gently press it onto the cake. Build up the full layer of hair all the way around before changing colour. Start each layer about 1.5 cm (³/₄ in.) higher than the last so you get an overlap of colour. Wash

the gun between different colours of fondant (see page 162).

### STEP 9

To paint the eyes, mix a tiny amount of the black powder with a drop of the clear alcohol or dipping solution in the paint palette. For each eye, first paint an oval outline, then, in the top right of the oval, draw the outline of a tiny rectangle. This will be the white area that makes the eyes look lifelike – as if the light is hitting them. Then fill in the rest of the eyes with the black paint.

### STEP 10

Insert the hands carefully, pushing the cocktail sticks into Mr Fluffles' body.

12

### FURTHERING YOUR SKILLS

When using the extruder gun, remember to make sure your fondant is really soft and pliable. Get the fondant warmed in your hands as this ensures it comes through the extruder gun really easily. Persevere with it – the whole process takes a little practise, but you will soon get the hang of it. I find washing the gun in hot water and filling it immediately with the next colour helps – the warmth keeps the fondant pliable.

### STEP 11

To make the eyes, roll two walnut-sized balls of white fondant and flatten them with your thumb. When you are half way up the cake, position the eyes on the side of the cake. They will stick on easily with just a small amount of pressure as the frosting will hold them in place.

### STEP 12

When you decorate the top of the cake, you will need to have the hair arranged in concentric circles around the centre of the head, each one in a different colour.

### STEP 13

For his antennae, take two small balls of each colour of fondant and roll them into a rough ball shape. Flatten each ball just a little.

### STEP 14

To fasten the balls in place, insert the remaining two cocktail sticks into the top of the cake. Dampen each ball slightly and thread them onto the sticks – the moisture will help them stick to each other.

# Eastern promise cake

This large intricate cake, decorated in warm jewel tones and embellished with luxurious gold lace, is perfect for a wedding. It would also work well for any large celebration as the cake serves more than an average single-tier dessert.

**SKILLS FOR REVIEW**
Filling and crumb coating a cake:
page 50
Covering a cake: page 58
Rolling out fondant and marzipan:
page 54
Dowelling a cake: page 62

## EQUIPMENT

Turntable

Embossing cutter set

Craft knife

2 fine paintbrushes, for gluing
and painting

Paint palette

## INGREDIENTS

8 cm (3 in.) round basic sponge cake
(see page 20)

13 cm (5 in.) round basic sponge cake

18 cm (7 in.) round basic sponge cake

3 quantities frosting in your chosen
colour and flavour (see page 28)

1 quantity fondant each in teal, pink,
purple and white (see page 34)

Edible glue (see page 41)

Lustre dust in gold

Clear alcohol or dipping solution

## FURTHERING YOUR SKILLS

While this cake and its warm tones are suitable for any colourful event, it would be equally as charming in subtle pastel hues.

## STEP 1

Using the frosting, fill and crumb coat each of the cakes, but don't stack them yet.

## STEP 2

Roll out the three bright fondant colours one by one and use them to cover each cake individually. Set aside to dry, then dowel the cakes together, ready to be decorated.

## STEP 3

Roll out the white fondant. Using the embossing cutters, cut out sections in the fondant. Cut some sections in half lengthwise and others widthwise.

## STEP 4

Immediately stick the pieces around the bottom of each tier with the edible glue. Continue cutting and sticking the pieces until both tiers are decorated. Set aside for the glue to dry.

## STEP 5

Mix a few drops of the clear alcohol or dipping solution with 1 teaspoon lustre dust in the paint palette and carefully paint the lace strips.

# Painted daisy cake

The dainty daisies and butterfly on this cake really bring it to life. Try this technique on cupcakes and larger cakes too – your guests will leave in awe of your skills.

**SKILLS FOR REVIEW**
Filling and crumb coating a cake: page 50
Covering a cake: page 58
Painting on fondant: page 164

## EQUIPMENT

10 cm (4 in.) round cake card

Butterfly plunger cutter

Cel former or drying foam

Paint palette

2 fine paintbrushes, for gluing and painting

## INGREDIENTS

10 cm (4 in.) round basic sponge cake (see page 20)

1 quantity frosting in your chosen colour and flavour (see page 28)

1 quantity fondant in pale blue (see page 34)

1 quantity gum paste in white (see page 36)

Extra white powder

Edible glue (see page 41)

Food colouring paste in green and yellow

Edible food pen in brown

Lustre dust in pearl

Clear alcohol or dipping solution

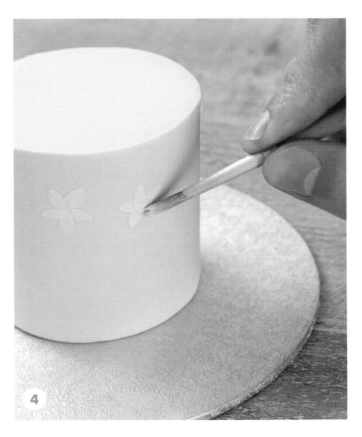

### STEP 1

Using the frosting, fill and crumb coat the cake. Then roll out the pale blue fondant and cover the cake.

### STEP 2

Knead the gum paste well and then roll it out until it is about 3 mm (⅛ in.) thick. Cut out a butterfly using the plunger cutter and place it in the cel former to set while you work on the rest of the cake.

### STEP 3

To paint the petals on the cake, mix a little of the extra white powder with a touch of corn flour and clear alcohol or dipping solution in the paint palette. Check the consistency by painting on a scrap of blue fondant. The paint should be easy to work with and a similar consistency to paints made using lustre dust. The paint should be smooth, so press out any lumps using the back of a teaspoon.

### STEP 4

To paint a petal, sweep across the surface with the whole length of the bristles, and lift when you reach the centre of where you want the daisy positioned. This will give you attractive petals with inward strokes on each one. Paint five petals all meeting in the middle to form a daisy shape. Do this many times across the cake surface.

### STEP 5

Let the petals dry, and then mix a few drops of the clear alcohol or dipping solution with 1/2 teaspoon green food colouring paste to make some green paint. Paint thin stems to the flowers. Use long sweeping strokes for the stems and make sure you do not paint them perfectly straight as this will not appear lifelike.

### STEP 6

To add leaves to the stems, make two arched lines toward each other, then fill in the middle of the leaf. As you move around the cake, try to vary the angle of the leaves. Once you get comfortable painting them, you can add small flicks to the end of the leaf. Let the cake dry for a few minutes.

### STEP 7

Take some yellow food colouring paste and paint the centre of each daisy with a circle to represent the pollen. Again, leave the cake to dry for a few minutes.

### STEP 8

Use the brown edible food pen to draw tiny dots around the edge of the daisy centres. Draw the dots in a random pattern rather than a plain circle so they look natural. Set the cake aside to dry completely.

9

**STEP 9**

Take the butterfly, and using a dry paintbrush, carefully dust the butterfly with the lustre dust to give it a pearlescent finish. Finally, glue the butterfly in place on the edge of the cake with edible glue.

# Cakes for children's parties

## Cow cupcakes

I love this cow cupcake and his cheeky smile. This design would be so much fun for a children's party.

**SKILLS FOR REVIEW**
Flat topping a cupcake: page 66
Rolling out fondant: page 54
Using the scriber tool: page 159

### EQUIPMENT

| | |
|---|---|
| 8.5 cm (3 ½ in.) diameter circle cutter | Fine paintbrush |
| 4 cm (1 ¾ in.) diameter circle cutter | Scriber tool |
| Ball tool | Palette knife |

### INGREDIENTS

12 cupcakes from the basic recipe (see page 23)

½ quantity fondant in white, flesh tone, black and brown (see page 34)

Edible glue (see page 41)

### STEP 1
Using the palette knife, flat top each cupcake, finishing with a circle of the white fondant cut out with the larger circle cutter.

### STEP 2
Roll out the flesh-tone paste, cut out a circle the same size as the top of the cupcake, then place the cutter one-third of the way across the circle and cut a section of the fondant. Attach this piece to the lower half of the cupcake to create the nose and mouth area.

### STEP 3
Using the smallest end of the ball tool, use a gentle circular motion to indent the oval nostrils.

### STEP 4
Use the small circular cutter to indent the mouth, then add dimples using the smallest end of the ball tool.

### STEP 5
Once your pink and white fondants are dry, you can add two small balls of black fondant for the eyes.

### STEP 6
To make the ears, cut out two circles using the small circle cutter, one in black and the other one in white. Pinch one side of each circle together.

### STEP 7
Glue each of the ears to the top of the cow's head with a gap between them.

### STEP 8
Take a pea-sized ball of brown paste, split it into two and then roll each ball on one side to create a horn shape. Try to keep the horns equal in size. Using the edible glue, stick each horn on the cow's face, just below the end of each ear.

### STEP 9
Take a pea-sized ball of black paste, separate it into three pieces and roll into three strands of hair. Use the same principle as the horns, but keep rolling until it is nice and thin. Glue the hair into the gap between the horns and use the scriber tool to style the hair gently.

> **FURTHERING YOUR SKILLS**
>
> To create different breeds of cow, change the colours of the fondant. For example, make a black and white Jersey cow or brown Australian Braford.

# Lenny the lion cupcakes

This king of the jungle will be a favourite among the little ones at every party.

### SKILLS FOR REVIEW
Flat topping a cupcake: page 66
Rolling out fondant: page 54
Using the scriber tool: page 159

## EQUIPMENT

Palette knife

8 cm (3 ¼ in.) diameter circle cutter

4 cm (1 ¾ in.) diameter circle cutter

Scriber tool

2 fine paintbrushes, for gluing and painting

Paint palette

Cocktail stick

## INGREDIENTS

12 cupcakes from the basic recipe (see page 23)

1 quantity frosting in brown (see page 28)

½ quantity fondant in white and two shades of brown (see page 34)

Edible glue (see page 41)

Food colouring powder in black

Clear alcohol or dipping solution

### STEP 1

Using the palette knife, flat top each cupcake, finishing with a circle of the lighter shade of brown fondant.

### STEP 2

Cut a second large circle from the darker coloured fondant, and then, using the smaller circle cutter, remove the centre of the circle and discard. The outer ring will be the lion's mane.

### STEP 3

Using one of the paintbrushes, add a little edible glue to the back of the second circle and attach it to the top of the cupcake. Gently smooth both the outer and inner edges to blend the two together.

### STEP 4

Use the scriber tool to scribe lines in the fondant, sweeping out from the inner edge of the mane. Do this both lightly and firmly to give plenty of texture to the

mane. If you go over the same area twice, you can create a realistic look to the fur. This should take you around 5 minutes to do properly. The longer you spend on the mane, the better it looks. Notice the difference in length of the fur; this is done by going over some areas repetitively.

### STEP 5

To make the eyes, roll out two pea-sized pieces of the white fondant until they look like tiny cylinders. Flatten them using your fingertip and secure in place using edible glue in the centre of the face.

### STEP 6

For the lion's cheeks, take two small marble-sized balls of the darker brown paste, and using the pad of your fingertip, push the balls flat. Add a touch of glue two-thirds of the way down the face on either side and attach the cheeks to the face. Smooth over gently with your fingertip. Use the tip of a cocktail stick to poke lots of indents on the cheeks.

## STEP 7

To make the nose, take half a pea-sized amount of black fondant in either shade. Roll the fondant into a small ball then use your thumb and first finger to gently pinch one side of the ball to give it a nice rounded triangle shape. Add a little glue to the back of the nose and attach it to the centre of the face between the eyes and just above the cheeks.

## STEP 8

Paint the top half of both eyes in black. Then add a pair of eyebrows and some whiskers.

## STEP 9

To help bring your character to life, take the tiniest pinch of white fondant and split it into two tiny balls. Pop a bit of glue on the back of each ball and attach to the eyes to give the illusion of light hitting the eyes.

### FURTHERING YOUR SKILLS

**Make Lenny the lion into Loretta the lioness by adding eyelashes and a hint of blush to her cheeks using edible lustre.**

# Monkey cupcakes

This cheeky chimp will make a great addition to any party, and guests of all ages will love her.

## SKILLS FOR REVIEW
Flat topping a cupcake: page 66
Rolling out fondant: page 54

## EQUIPMENT

Palette knife

8 cm (3 ¼ in.) diameter circle cutter

Craft knife

2 cm (¾ in.) diameter circle cutter

1 cm (½ in.) diameter circle cutter

2 fine paintbrushes, for gluing and painting

Small blossom plunger cutter

## INGREDIENTS

12 cupcakes from the basic recipe (see page 23)

1 quantity frosting in your chosen colour and flavour (see page 28)

½ quantity fondant in brown, flesh tone and pink (see page 34)

Edible glue (see page 41)

Food colouring paste in black

Lustre dust in pink

Edible pearl, to decorate

### STEP 1

Using the palette knife, flat top each cupcake, finishing with a circle of the brown fondant cut out with the largest circle cutter.

### STEP 2

Roll out the flesh tone fondant and cut another circle, again with the larger cutter. Then use the craft knife to trim the circle to the face shape. Lay the face onto the cupcake and attach with edible glue.

### STEP 3

To make the ears, roll out a small piece of the brown fondant and cut out two circles, this time with the middle-sized cutter. Then roll out some more of the flesh tone fondant and cut out two circles with the smallest cutter. Stick the smaller circles on top of the bigger ones with edible glue and then stick them to either side of the face. Gently fold the ears back on themselves, so they stand proud from the cupcake.

### STEP 4

Make two tiny black fondant eyes, then paint three flicks for eye lashes on each. Then add in a cheeky smile on the side and three freckles on each cheek. The nose is painted as a small triangle with rounded edges. I have left a small dot on the top right of the nose unpainted to give the effect of the light reflecting.

### STEP 5

Finally, roll out the pink paste and cut a flower using the blossom plunger cutter. Glue it to the top right of the face and add the pearl to the centre. Dust a little pink lustre dust on each cheek to finish.

---

### FURTHERING YOUR SKILLS

For a cheekier monkey, dispense with the flower and blush, and add a bow tie or party hat in their place.

# Pirate cupcakes

'Ah ha me hearties!' This little pirate is sure to have you scrubbing the decks and walking the plank at every party.

### SKILLS FOR REVIEW
Flat topping a cupcake: page 66
Rolling out fondant: page 54
Using the scriber tool: page 159

## EQUIPMENT

Palette knife

8 cm (3 ¼ in.) diameter circle cutter

Craft knife

Fine paintbrush, for gluing

Balling tool

2 cm (⅗₄ in.) diameter circle cutter

Scriber tool

## INGREDIENTS

12 cupcakes from the basic recipe (see page 23)

1 quantity frosting in your chosen colour and flavour (see page 28)

½ quantity fondant in flesh tone, red, white and black (see page 34)

Edible glue (see page 41)

Edible food pen in black

## STEP 1

Using the palette knife, flat top each cupcake, finishing with a circle of the flesh tone fondant.

## STEP 2

Roll out the red fondant and cut out a circle, again using the large cutter. Then use the craft knife to cut the circle in half. Lay half of the red fondant over half of the cupcake to make a bandana and attach it with edible glue.

## STEP 3

Take a pea-sized ball of red fondant, roll it into a small cylinder shape, and then fold both ends over on themselves to give the impression of a knot. Attach this to the side of the bandana with a little edible glue.

## STEP 4

Now take half a pea-sized bit of the flesh tone fondant and roll it into a ball. Then, using the scribe tool, pick it up and attach to the side of the face just under the bandana knot for an ear. Roll another tiny ball of flesh fondant and glue it in the centre of the face for the nose.

## STEP 5

To make an eye, add one tiny ball of the black fondant just above and to the left of the nose. To make the eye patch, roll out a small piece of the black fondant and cut a circle using the smaller cutter. Then use the craft knife to cut it in half to make a patch. Glue it in place of the other eye, making sure the edge lines up with the edge of the bandana.

## STEP 6

Using the scriber tool, mark a small curved smile to one side and a little dot at each end to give him dimples. Add three freckles to each cheek in a triangle.

## STEP 7

Finally, roll seven tiny balls of the white fondant and add them to the bandana and flatten with your fingertip.

---

### FURTHERING YOUR SKILLS

**Change the little pirate to a girl by adding a pink or yellow bandana and some pink lustre dust to her cheeks.**

# Viking cupcakes

*This brave warrior will win over the hearts of anyone he meets.*

**SKILLS FOR REVIEW**
Flat topping a cupcake: page 66
Rolling out fondant: page 54
Using the scriber tool: page 159

## EQUIPMENT

*Palette knife*

*8 cm (3 ¼ in.) diameter circle cutter*

*Craft knife*

*2 fine paintbrushes for gluing and painting*

*Wilton No. 1 round decorating tip*

*Scriber tool*

## INGREDIENTS

*12 cupcakes from the basic recipe (see page 23)*

*1 quantity frosting in your chosen colour and flavour (see page 28)*

*½ quantity fondant in skin tone, orange, white and gray (see page 34)*

*Edible glue (see page 41)*

*Food colouring paste in black*

### STEP 1
Using the palette knife, flat top each cupcake, finishing with a 8 cm (3 ¼ in.) diameter circle cut out of the flesh tone fondant.

### STEP 2
Roll out the gray fondant and cut out another circle from it. Use the craft knife to slice this circle in half. Set aside one half.

### STEP 3
Use the craft knife to cut a thin strip from the straight edge of the remaining gray semicircle. Set this aside to dry, and then attach the remaining part of the semicircle to one side of the cupcake to form the helmet.

### STEP 4
Lay the thin strip over the helmet along the edge and stick in place with edible glue. Take the rest of the gray semicircle, and cut out a vertical strip. Attach it to the centre of the helmet with edible glue.

### STEP 5
Press the very small piping tip gently along both of the thin strips on the helmet. This will give the appearance of rivets in the helmet.

### STEP 6

To make the beard, roll out the orange fondant and cut out a circle using the cutter. Take the craft knife and cut away the majority of the fondant circle to leave you with a rounded beard shape. Stick this to the bottom of the face.

### STEP 7

Use the scriber tool to scribe in a smile in the centre of the beard.

### STEP 8

Take a small piece of the leftover flesh tone fondant to shape a small nose and attach it to the centre of the face. I have gone for a small triangular nose, but you can

choose any shape of nose to give him his own character. A teardrop shape will give him a more rounded nose, for example.

### STEP 9

Take two tiny balls of white fondant and attach them on either side at the top of the nose. Then use the black food colouring paste and paintbrush to paint the pupils on the eyes and two fine eyebrows.

## FURTHERING YOUR SKILLS

- Try making different styled beards to give your Viking a whole new look. Try a long pointed one or perhaps a moustache but no beard.

- Turn Harold into Helga by removing the beard and adding blond curls made with an extruder gun before applying her helmet (see page 162).

# Festive cupcakes

## Christmas pudding cupcakes

Christmas would not be complete without a Christmas pudding cupcake. The large dome of frosting makes this the ideal cupcake to have as dessert with family and friends.

**SKILLS FOR REVIEW**
Flat topping a cupcake: page 66
Rolling out fondant: page 54
Using the scriber tool: page 159

### EQUIPMENT

10 cm (4 in.) diameter circle cutter

5-petal cutter

Holly plunger cutter

Fine paintbrush, for gluing

Palette knife

### INGREDIENTS

12 cupcakes from the basic recipe (see page 23)

1 quantity frosting in your chosen colour and flavour (see page 28)

½ quantity fondant in brown, red, white and green (see page 34)

Edible glue (see page 41)

## STEP 1
Use the palette knife to build a dome of frosting gradually on top of the cupcake. You are looking for a dome that is around 3.5 cm (1 ½ in.) higher than the edge of the cupcake case.

## STEP 2
Roll out the brown fondant to 3 mm (⅛ in.) thick and cut out a circle using the cutter. Place the circle over the dome of frosting and smooth down gently at the edges.

## STEP 3
Roll out the white fondant until it is 3 mm (⅛ in.) thick and cut a shape using the 5-petal cutter. This will become the frosting on top of the pudding.

## STEP 4
Attach the white frosting section to the brown pudding section with edible glue.

## STEP 5
Roll out the green fondant out until it is around 2 mm (¹⁄₁₀ in.) thick. Use the holly plunger cutter to cut and emboss the shape. Attach this to the centre of the cupcake dome with edible glue.

## STEP 6
Roll three tiny red berries from the red fondant. These should be very small so that they fit with the size of the holly. Attach them to the centre of the holly with edible glue to finish the cupcake.

### FURTHERING YOUR SKILLS
**Use the palm of your hand to polish the brown fondant as you smooth down the edges to give it a really glossy finish.**

# Robin cupcakes

Even Scrooge could not resist Christmas with these little cuties at the table.

## SKILLS FOR REVIEW
Flat topping a cupcake: page 66
Rolling out fondant: page 54
Using the scriber tool: page 159

## EQUIPMENT

Palette knife

8 cm (3 ¼ in.) diameter circle cutter

Scriber tool

Fine paintbrush, for gluing

## INGREDIENTS

12 cupcakes from the basic recipe (see page 23)

Edible glue (see page 41)

1 quantity frosting in your chosen colour and flavour (see page 28)

½ quantity fondant in brown, red, orange and black (see page 34)

## STEP 1

Using the palette knife, flat top each cupcake, finishing with a circle of the brown fondant. Then, using your index finger, smooth down the lower side of the cupcake and round off the higher side, to form a rounded stomach.

## STEP 2

Roll out the red fondant and cut out another circle. Move the cutter half way across the circle and press down again. This will leave you with a rugby ball shape of red fondant, which will be the robin's red breast. Dampen the reverse of the red shape with a little glue and attach it over the rounded stomach.

## STEP 3

To make the bird's beak, roll a small pea-sized ball of the orange fondant into a cone and fix in the middle of the cupcake at the join between the red and brown sections.

## STEP 4

Roll two more pea-sized balls of the orange fondant into small cylinders. Use the scriber tool to make two indentations across each and affix them to the base of the bird under his stomach with edible glue.

## STEP 5

To make the eyes, you need a pea-sized piece of the black fondant. Split it into two pieces and roll them into balls before sticking into place on either side of the beak.

## STEP 6

Finally, make the wings from two gobstopper-sized pieces of the brown fondant. Flatten them both with your finger until they are wing shaped, then stick the wings in place on either side of the bird with edible glue.

### FURTHERING YOUR SKILLS

**To create a beautiful love bird, change the colours of this robin from brown to blue and make a pink chest – ideal for many occasions.**

# Sport-themed cupcakes

## Tennis ball cupcakes

From the US Open to Wimbledon, everyone loves tennis, and these cupcakes are perfect to munch your way through after – or even during – the match.

**SKILLS FOR REVIEW**
Rolling out fondant: page 54
Using foam drying balls: page 156
Using an extruder gun: page 162

### EQUIPMENT

10 cm (4 in.) diameter circle cutter

Foam drying balls

Extruder gun

Fine paintbrush, for gluing

Palette knife

### INGREDIENTS

12 cupcakes from the basic recipe (see page 23)

½ quantity fondant in yellow and white (see page 34)

Edible glue (see page 41)

Frosting in your chosen colour and flavour (see page 28)

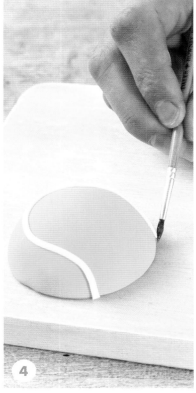

### STEP 1

Roll out the yellow fondant until it is about 3 mm (⅛ in.) thick and cut out a circle using the cutter. Lay it over one of the foam drying balls and smooth down to create a dome.

### STEP 2

Insert the small single circular hole disc in the extruder gun and then fill it with a piece of the white fondant. Squeeze a long length of the white fondant through the gun on to your work surface. If you don't have an extruder gun, roll out the white fondant to about 3 mm (⅛ in.) thick and use a ruler and sharp knife to carefully cut a 5 mm (¼ in.) wide strip of the fondant.

### STEP 3

Using the edible glue, paint a line on the yellow fondant dome that resembles the looped line on a tennis ball.

### STEP 4

Lay the white strip over the glued area and gently smooth the line using your finger to make it more flat than round. Set the dome aside for about 30 minutes to set.

### STEP 5

When you are ready to finish decorating the cupcake, use the palette knife to build a small dome of frosting on the top of your cupcake and then carefully place the dome of fondant on the top.

# Basketball cupcakes

You cannot score a slam dunk with these cupcakes, and I doubt they would bounce well, but they are always a big hit with the fans.

### SKILLS FOR REVIEW
Rolling out fondant: page 54
Using foam drying balls: page 156

## EQUIPMENT

10 cm (4 in.) diameter circle cutter

Foam drying balls

Craft knife

Fine paintbrush, for gluing

Palette knife

## INGREDIENTS

12 cupcakes from the basic recipe (see page 23)

½ quantity fondant in orange and black
   (see page 34)

Edible glue (see page 41)

1 quantity frosting in your chosen colour and flavour
   (see page 28)

### STEP 1
Roll out both of the fondant colours until they are about 3 mm (⅛ in.) thick and cut out a circle from the orange colour using the cutter. Lay it over one of the foam drying balls and smooth down to create a dome.

### STEP 2
Cut two long thin strips out of the black fondant using the craft knife.

### STEP 3
Using the edible glue, paint a cross and then two outward arc lines on the top of the dome. Attach the black strips and gently smooth them in place. Set the dome aside for about 30 minutes to set.

### STEP 4
When you are ready to finish decorating the cupcake, use the palette knife to build a small dome of frosting on the top of your cupcake and then carefully place the dome of fondant on the top.

### FURTHERING YOUR SKILLS
Use this technique to make a golf ball instead of a basketball. Once you have placed the white fondant over the dome, use a ball tool to make dimples across the surface of the fondant for the perfect golf ball finish.

# Baseball cupcakes

*All those little leaguers will love this treat after a game.*

### SKILLS FOR REVIEW
**Rolling out fondant: page 54**
**Using foam drying balls: page 156**

## EQUIPMENT

*10 cm (4 in.) diameter circle cutter*

*Foam drying balls*

*Wilton No. 1 round decorating tip*

*Piping bag*

*Palette knife*

## INGREDIENTS

*12 cupcakes from the basic recipe (see page 23)*

*1 quantity royal icing in red (see page 40)*

*1 quantity frosting in your chosen colour and flavour
    (see page 28)*

*½ quantity fondant in white (see page 34)*

### STEP 1
Roll out the white fondant until it is about 3 mm (⅛ in.) thick and cut out a circle using the cutter. Lay it over one of the foam drying balls and smooth down to create a dome. Using the circle cutter, indent an arc on each side of the dome.

### STEP 2
Secure the tip in your piping bag, then fill it with the red royal icing and pipe baseball stitches along each side of the indentations. Set the dome aside for about 30 minutes to set.

### STEP 3
When you are ready to finish decorating the cupcake, use the palette knife to build a small dome of frosting on the top of your cupcake and place the dome of fondant on the top.

### FURTHERING YOUR SKILLS

**With other sports you may use the same techniques as used here, just adjust the detailing accordingly. For example, for a football, emboss hexagons into the fondant dome rather than indenting arcs, and then paint them to represent a football.**

# Working with gum paste

When you are making decorations for cakes, you need them to remain firm and hold their shape. This is a good time to use gum paste. Gum paste has different properties than fondant. It is a strong material that holds its shape no matter how thin you roll it. It is ideal for creating three-dimensional shapes. Gum paste is made from fondant with the addition of CMC powder, which is the strengthening agent (see page 36 for the recipe).

# Gum paste or fondant?

You may think that you can only use fondant when covering cakes and that gum paste is for decorations and figures. However, there are times when you may need to use gum paste to help decorate the cake itself. Here are some examples of when gum paste is easier to use than fondant.

### STEP 1

When you are working with shapes, you may find regular fondant stretches and loses it shape when hung vertically. Use gum paste and let the shapes firm up for about 10 minutes before adding them to the cake.

### STEP 2

When you are covering cupcakes with domes made on foam drying balls (see page 156), making them from gum paste means they set faster – ideal for those days when you are in a hurry.

### STEP 3

For cakes such as the Fabric Effect Clutch Bag (see page 234), gum paste will allow you to achieve thinner ruffles, and they will also hold their shape much better.

---

#### FURTHERING YOUR SKILLS

Sometimes it is better not to use gum paste as it would be too firm for a whole cake covering. However, it is worth remembering that you can add just a half or quarter measurement of CMC powder to your fondant if it is too soft. Unlike gum paste, it will not set solid, but it will help you to achieve the cake covering you need.

# Achieving a good modelling consistency

Gum paste is a great medium when used correctly. However, there are times when you may find your models cracking and breaking. Here are some tips to ensure this does not happen to your designs.

**STEP 1**

Before using the gum paste, knead it well until it takes on a warm gum-like texture. The paste should be stretchy and pliable.

**STEP 2**

To keep the paste from drying out, wrap it well in cling film and store in an airtight container until needed.

**STEP 3**

Use only the amount you need each time. The rest of the paste should be left in the cling film to keep it moist. Sometimes, when you are modelling, you may find that certain tasks take longer than expected. The excess paste will begin to dry out if you do not wrap it in cling film.

**STEP 4**

If your paste is too moist, roll it in some corn flour to help it return to a workable state. Conversely, if you notice the paste is too dry, rub a little vegetable shortening between your hands and knead the paste until it becomes moist again and easier to work with.

## FURTHERING YOUR SKILLS

When modelling figures, remember that the gum paste is heavy. You may need to use supports, such as spaghetti, to prevent arms falling off or your figures leaning.

# Using cutters and moulds

Gum paste is so versatile that you can use it with the most intricate moulds and cutters. It takes on the fine detail of the mould it is in very well. You will achieve results that would be impossible with basic fondant.

### STEP 1

When you are using cutters with gum paste, make sure you cut through the paste cleanly to get a crisp edge to the shape. If you are drying a three-dimensional flower or other item, use a cel former to help the item hold its shape.

### STEP 2

Dust a mould with corn flour before inserting the gum paste as this will help the dried gum paste release more easily.

### STEP 3

To make well-defined shapes, use a ball tool to push the paste into the tiny crevices in the mould before filling the main body so that all the detail will be visible when it is released.

### STEP 4

Humidity can affect the time it takes for the gum paste to set in the moulds. So if you want to speed things up or you are having trouble removing gum paste shapes from daintier moulds, put the filled mould in the freezer for about 10 minutes until it is solid. Remove the mould from the freezer and release the piece immediately. The paste will return to room temperature slowly and may appear wet for some time. Don't panic – this is normal.

**EQUIPMENT**

| | |
|---|---|
| Cutters | Mould |
| Cel former or drying foam | Ball tool |

# Making a ribbon rose

Sometimes you want a decoration that is a little less formal than a dainty rose to adorn your cakes. The ribbon rose is a softer, rounded style and ideal as a replacement for traditional roses.

## EQUIPMENT

*Craft knife*

*Cel former or drying foam*

### STEP 1

Take a walnut-sized piece of gum paste and make sure it is warm and stretchy. Then roll it out into a rectangle slightly larger than 4 x 12 cm (4 ¾ x 1 ¾ in.) and about 2 mm (¹/₁₆ in.) thick. The thinner this is, the better the flower will look. Using the craft knife, trim the edges to neaten.

### STEP 2

Bring the two longest outer edges together and gently smooth the gum paste down so you have the folded edge at the top.

### STEP 3

Gently fold over the smooth corner of the gum paste at one end to meet the base rough edge and create a triangle. This will leave you with a smooth rounded edge and this will become the centre of your rose.

### STEP 4

Roll the triangle end over one full turn to create the bud of the rose.

### STEP 5

Carefully lift the gum paste and begin to turn the rose bud toward the rest of the paste. With each turn, gather and pinch the gum paste to loosen up the rose shape and give it a fabric effect.

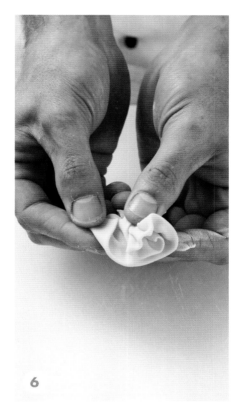

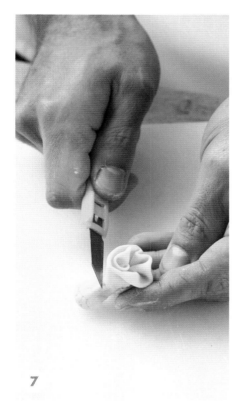

5

6

7

## STEP 6

As you reach the end of the gum paste, tuck the final piece downwards to hide where the rose finishes.

## STEP 7

Use the craft knife to remove the excess from the back of the rose. This will enable you to attach it closer to the cake you are decorating. Set the rose aside to dry in the cel former for about 30 minutes.

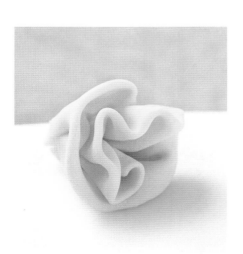

# Making a corsage

This beautiful cake decoration is a variation on the ribbon rose, see page 209, but these three flowers of different sizes group together on top of a cake for the perfect corsage effect. There is also a small hint of colour in the centre of each flower.

**SKILLS FOR REVIEW**
Two-tier Wedding Cake: page 248

## EQUIPMENT

Craft knife

Cel former or drying foam

Scriber tool

Edible pearls (optional)

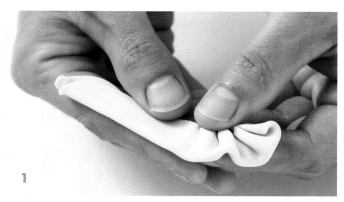

### STEP 1

Follow steps 1–7, as for Ribbon Rose, page 209, but unlike the ribbon rose, keep the shape flat.

### STEP 2

Make a slightly smaller flower in the same way to sit in the middle of the larger one. Stick the smaller flower inside the larger one and then set it aside to dry in the cel former for about 30 minutes.

### STEP 3

Repeat Steps 1 and 2, making a slightly smaller flower. Set the two flowers aside to dry.

### STEP 4

Group the flowers on the cake you are decorating to make one whole corsage and stick it in place with a little edible glue. Then make a small gobstopper-sized ball of a contrasting colour of paste and glue it to the centre of the corsage. Use the scriber tool to mark a cross across the ball. Alternatively, cover the centre ball in edible pearls.

# Making a ruffle

The narrow strip of gum paste that is stuck over the main part of the ruffle hides a myriad of sins. One rectangle that is 51 cm (20 in.) long, ends up being about 25 cm (10 in.) once it is pleated.

**SKILLS FOR REVIEW**
Two-tier Wedding Cake: page 248

**EQUIPMENT**

*Craft knife*

*Ruler*

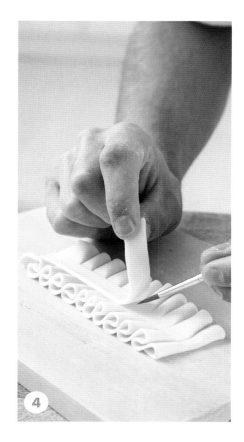

## STEP 1

Roll out the gum paste until it is very thin, then use the craft knife and ruler to cut out a rectangle measuring 5 x 51 cm (2 x 20 in.).

## STEP 2

Gather the ruffle, pressing it in the centre to hold. Once you have gathered it all, use your thumb to smooth the centre of the ruffle and make sure there are no bumps.

## STEP 3

Roll out more of the gum paste, and use the craft knife to cut out a 1–2 cm (½–¾ in.) wide strip that is long enough to cover the length of the ruffle.

## STEP 4

Stick the strip along the centre of the ruffle with edible glue, making sure it is perfectly straight.

# Cake toppers

## Rabbit cake topper

This young rabbit will look perfect on top of children's cakes and Easter celebration cakes.

1

**SKILLS FOR REVIEW**
Achieving a good modelling
consistency: page 207
Using the scriber tool: page 159

### EQUIPMENT

Scriber tool

2 fine paintbrushes, for gluing
    and painting

Piece of uncooked spaghetti

Craft knife

Paint palette

### INGREDIENTS

1 quantity gum paste in beige, pale
    beige and pink (see page 36)

Edible glue (see page 41)

Food colouring paste in black

Clear alcohol or dipping solution

Lustre dust in pink

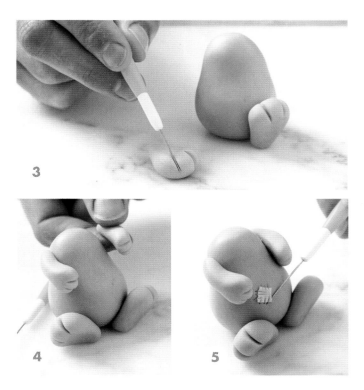

## STEP 1

To start making the rabbit, roll a golf ball-sized piece of the beige gum paste and then press in the middle to give you a small indentation. Then roll one side slightly thinner and stand it on its end. You now have the rabbit's body with a suitably saggy tummy.

## STEP 2

To make the arms and legs, take four gobstopper-sized pieces of the beige gum paste and roll them into balls. Rolling carefully on one side, create a rounded point on one end. They will look like teardrops when they are ready.

## STEP 3

Stick two of the teardrops under the front of the rabbit's tummy using the edible glue. Then use the scriber tool to add two lines to each foot to delineate the toes.

## STEP 4

Stick the other two pieces as arms on either side of the rabbit. Use the scriber to add two small lines on the paws.

## STEP 5

Roll out another small piece of the pale beige paste and use the craft knife to cut a tiny square measuring about 5 x 5 mm (¼ x ¼ in.). Attach to the rabbit's tummy and then use the scriber tool to mark stitches on each side.

## STEP 6

Roll a small ball of beige paste for the rabbit's head. Add a tiny ball of the pale beige gum paste to the face as the cheeks, then use the scriber tool to indent the top of the cheeks a little so you can insert a nose. Also use the pointed end of the scriber tool to scribe in a vertical line and flick out to each side for a wide smile.

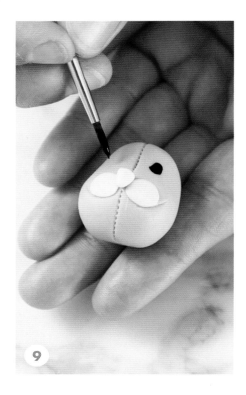

## STEP 7

Roll a very tiny ball of the pink gum paste and glue it in the hole you have made at the top of the cheeks. Use your fingertips to smooth the ball into a flat button nose.

## STEP 8

Use the stitching tool to mark a line down the centre of the rabbit's tummy and up and over its head too to give him an authentic, stitched look.

## STEP 9

Mix a small amount of the black food colouring paste with a few drops of the clear alcohol or dipping solution in the paint palette and then carefully paint two little round dots for the eyes and make three small flicks outwards for the eyelashes.

## STEP 10

Insert a stick of spaghetti into the body of the rabbit and then place the head on top. Add a touch of glue where the head and body meet to give the join added strength.

## STEP 11

To finish the rabbit, dip a dry paintbrush into the lustre dust and add a little pink to both cheeks.

### FURTHERING YOUR SKILLS

**Change the colour of the fabric patch to make a more male- or female-oriented design.**

# Fairy cake topper

This pretty fairy will look great sitting on top of a cake or cupcake with her elegant chignon and delicate wings.

## SKILLS FOR REVIEW
Achieving a good modelling consistency: page 207
Using the scriber tool: page 159
Using cutters and moulds: page 208

## EQUIPMENT

Head mould

10 cm (4 in.) diameter circle cutter

2 fine paintbrushes, for gluing
    and painting

Craft knife

Scriber tool

Piece of uncooked spaghetti

Balling tool

Paint palette

Butterfly plunger cutter

Cel former or drying foam

## INGREDIENTS

1 quantity gum paste in flesh
    tone, pink, white and brown
    (see page 36)

Edible glue (see page 41)

Food colouring paste in brown and red

Clear alcohol or dipping solution

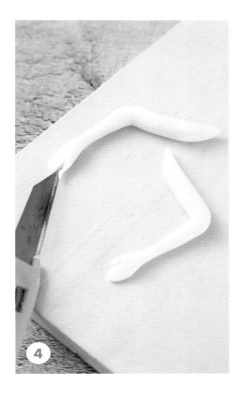

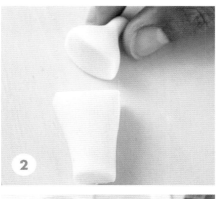

### STEP 1

Using a head mould, make a head out of flesh tone paste and leave to dry. Model two thin cylinders of the same paste for the fairy's legs. Pinch the bottom of each leg flat and then turn it upwards by 45 degrees to become the foot.

### STEP 2

Take a golf ball-sized piece of the pink gum paste and model it into a cone shape with a flattened tip. This will become the fairy's body. Take a gobstopper-sized piece of flesh tone fondant and make a shorter cone, rolling one end to become her neck. Attach to the body using a little glue and a piece of uncooked spaghetti.

### STEP 3

Now roll out most of the pink paste and cut out a circle using the cutter. Put a little glue under the body and then stick the circle of paste under it. Gather the paste to look like a dress.

### STEP 4

Model the arms separately out of the flesh tone paste. Model two thin cylinders. This time when you flatten the end of each one to make the hands, use the craft knife to cut a small triangle of paste from each hand to give them thumbs. Then add three lines for the fingers.

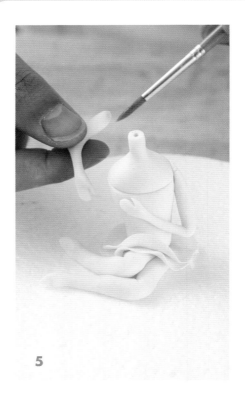

## STEP 5

Stick each arm in place, and pose them as you'd like.

## STEP 6

Use a little more of the pink paste to make two dress straps. Roll out to make two tiny cylinders, and glue in place over the seam where the arm meets the shoulder.

## STEP 7

Add a piece of spaghetti to the top of the body to hold the head. Surround the piece of spaghetti with some glue to help it stick. The moulded head should be dry by now and ready to work with.

## STEP 8

To make the hair, roll lots of thin strips from the brown paste and twist them into spirals as you stick them in place with glue.

## STEP 9

To make the ears, roll two tiny balls of the flesh tone paste and use the balling tool to pick two of them up. Add a dab of glue on either side of the face and press the ears in place.

## STEP 10

Using brown food colouring, paint eye and eyebrow details onto the fairy's face. Then use red food colouring to paint in her lips. Set the fairy aside to dry for about

5 minutes to keep the colour from bleeding. Then add the head to the body, adding a little edible glue around the spaghetti to strengthen the join. Set aside to dry for 30 minutes.

### STEP 11
Now for the fairy's wings: Roll out the remaining white paste to about 3 mm (1/8 in.) thick and cut out a butterfly using the plunger tool. Leave this to dry in the cel former.

### STEP 12
Finally, stick the wings in place on the back of the fairy and place her on the top of your cake.

---

### FURTHERING YOUR SKILLS
**Make sure you let your fairy dry completely before you try to move her.**

# Baby figure

I love this sweet little baby, it's so adaptable from boys to girls and looks beautiful resting on any cake. I have made this project as simple as possible because I know so many people are daunted by making figures.

**SKILLS FOR REVIEW**
Achieving a good modelling
consistency: page 207

### EQUIPMENT

Craft knife

Piece of uncooked spaghetti

2 fine paintbrushes

Stitching tool

Paint palette

### INGREDIENTS

1 quantity gum paste in pink, brown, white and flesh tone (see page 36)

Edible glue (see page 41)

Lustre dusts in blue and brown

Clear alcohol or dipping solution

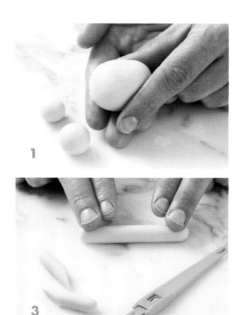

### STEP 1

Shape a walnut-sized piece of pink paste into a large body, then make two smaller balls, which will form the arms and legs. One ball should be slightly bigger than the other.

### STEP 2

Using the paste for the body, make a cylinder shape, then turn it vertically and push it down onto the work surface to give it a flat bottom. Use your thumb and forefinger to squeeze the sides gently at the base and then again near the top. This will give somewhere flat for the arms and legs to be attached.

### STEP 3

Take the two balls of paste and roll both out into long cylinder shapes. Then, using the craft knife, cut diagonally across each piece of paste. This will give you a good flat surface for attaching the arms and legs to the body. Turn them so you have a left and right side.

### STEP 4

Use the bottom of the paintbrush to make an indentation in the bottom of each arm to create a hole to insert the hands.

### STEP 5

Take the larger lengths and mould the legs. Curve them to give the baby a knee. Using a craft knife, trim off the end where the ankle is.

### STEP 6

Add a dab of glue to the inside of the arms and legs and then attach them to the baby's body. Remember to leave enough room for the hands between the arms.

### STEP 7

For the hands and feet, take four pea-sized balls of the flesh tone fondant. Roll one end of the balls to create a teardrop shape, then flatten the tear drops to create the hands and feet.

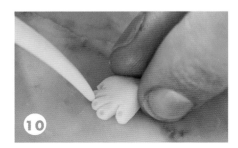

### STEP 8
Use the craft knife to remove a small triangle of paste from each hand to give them thumbs. Then cut three more vertical lines to make the fingers. Do the same for toes.

### STEP 9
Round the ends of the fingers. If you separate the fingers well, this will be easier. If you need to add more pressure, you can, but pressing too hard will squish the fingers. It does take a bit of practise. Remember, though, that if you go wrong you can roll them up and start again.

### STEP 10
Take the scriber tool and gently press it into the tip of each finger to give the baby fingernails.

### STEP 11
Paint a small amount of edible glue around the wrist of each hand, gently push them inside the arms, and pose the hands however you would like.

### STEP 12
Using the stitching tool, roll it straight down the front of the body and make indents for buttons.

### STEP 13
Now you can move onto the head, which will need fixing in place with a piece of spaghetti as well as edible glue. Hold the spaghetti vertically behind the baby's body and measure from its bottom to 3 cm (1 1/4 in.) above the top of the body. Break the spaghetti at this point and insert it into the top of the body and push it down.

### STEP 14
To make the head, take a large ball of flesh tone fondant. The size of the head should be in proportion to the body, so judge this by eye when deciding if it is big enough.

### STEP 15
Take the ball, and gently use one finger to roll it on one side and make an attractive head shape. Place the head on your cel former to make it easier to work with.

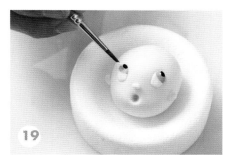

## STEP 16

Make the baby's mouth by inserting the end of the paintbrush. Take the tiny amount of white paste and roll into a small cylinder, and then flatten it. Cut the cylinder in half with the craft knife so that you have two eyes. Using a small dab of glue, attach them to the head.

## STEP 17

For the nose and ears, take a pea-sized piece of flesh fondant and split it into three equal parts. Roll them into balls, and attach one as the nose with edible glue.

## STEP 18

Use the tip of your paintbrush to pick up the other two balls, one at a time, and position them as ears. The paintbrush tip will give a circular hole to the ears. Then gently, use the tip of your finger to press together the base of each ear for a realistic shape.

## STEP 19

Take a small amount of both the brown and blue powdered colours and add them to the paint palette. Add two drops of the clear alcohol or dipping solution to each and mix into paint. Use a separate brush for each colour. Load your brush with blue paint and fill in the eyes. If you want to achieve a bright colour, do two layers of paint.

## STEP 20

Switch to brown paint and add the eyebrows. Using a separate paintbrush, add a little pink lustre to the cheeks.

## STEP 21

For the baby's curl, take a piece of brown paste half the size of a pea and roll into a thin cylinder, then roll one end into a point. Dab some glue where you want the curl to go on the top of the baby's head. Attach the thick end of the hair to the head, then twist the rest into a spiral to achieve the cutest curl.

# Celebration party cake

This is a great all-around party cake and also serves as an ideal last-minute gift.

**SKILLS FOR REVIEW**
Filling and crumb coating
a cake: page 50
Covering a cake: page 58
Using cutters and moulds: page 208

## EQUIPMENT

Large star cutters

Star plunger cutters

Craft knife

Jumbo straws

Fine paintbrush, for gluing

## INGREDIENTS

18 cm (7 in.) round basic sponge cake (see page 20)

1 quantity frosting in your chosen colour and flavour (see page 28)

1 quantity white fondant (see page 34)

1 quantity gum paste in 4 bright colours (see page 36)

Edible glue (see page 41)

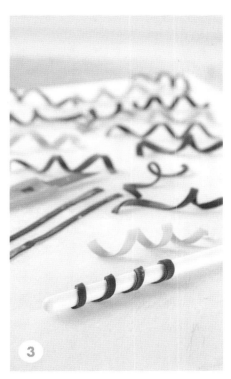

### STEP 1

Using the frosting, fill and crumb coat the cake. Then roll out the white fondant and cover the cake.

### STEP 2

Roll out the various colours of gum paste and cut out ten stars of varying sizes in each colour. Set them aside on a flat surface to dry.

### STEP 3

To make streamers, gather up the remains of the gum paste (keeping each colour separate) and roll out again. Using the craft knife, cut out five 5 mm (¼ in.) wide strips of each colour, then wind the strips around the jumbo straws and set aside to dry.

### STEP 4

Remove the straws from the gum paste streamers and stick them on the top of the cake with edible glue.

### STEP 5

For the final decorations, stick the stars in trails around the side of the cake and stand a few of them on the top of the cake by pressing one point into the surface.

---

### FURTHERING YOUR SKILLS

**Make this cake in black with the stars and streamers in metallic colours and you will have the perfect New Year's Eve cake.**

# Nest cake

This cake is adorable and ideal for a baby shower, christening, child's birthday or Easter.

**SKILLS FOR REVIEW**
Filling and crumb coating
a cake: page 50
Covering a cake: page 58
Using cutters and moulds: page 208
Using an extruder gun: page 162

## EQUIPMENT

Middle-sized cutter, from the PME set of circle plunger cutters

Extruder gun

Craft knife

Fine paintbrush, for gluing

Palette knife

## INGREDIENTS

18 cm (7 in.) round basic sponge cake (see page 20)

1 quantity frosting in your chosen colour and flavour (see page 28)

1 quantity yellow fondant (see page 34)

1 ½ quantities gum paste in lilac, brown, pink, blue and orange (see page 36)

Edible glue (see page 41)

Edible food pen in black

## STEP 1

Using the frosting, fill and crumb coat the cake. Then roll out the yellow fondant and cover the cake.

## STEP 2

Roll out the lilac gum paste, and use the circle plunger to cut out about 30 circles. Stick these all over the cake in a random pattern.

## STEP 3

Knead the brown gum paste until it is really soft. Insert the largest multiple-hole disc in the extruder gun and then fill it with the brown paste. Push out the paste, which will look like pieces of spaghetti, and immediately start twisting it into a nest shape. Build up the shape until you are happy with it, then leave it to dry for 30 minutes.

## STEP 4

To make the birds, roll walnut-sized balls from the pink and blue gum pastes. Then roll each ball on one side to create a cone. Use your fingertips to curve up the tip of the cone, then flatten it gently.

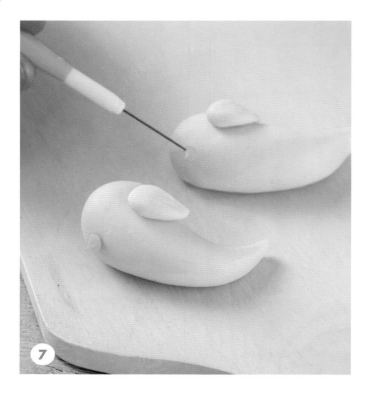

## STEP 5
Use the craft knife to cut two lines in the tail to separate it into three segments.

## STEP 6
For the wings, roll out two smaller cones of the pink and blue gum paste. Flatten them both with your fingertips and then gently add three lines on the edge of each wing. Attach the wings to the birds using edible glue.

## STEP 7
Roll two tiny balls of the yellow paste then pinch them into a beak shape. Stick them in place on each bird with the edible glue, then add two tiny dots to each bird for the eyes using the edible food pen.

## STEP 8
Move the nest onto the cake and secure it in place with edible glue. To finish, place one bird in the nest and the other beside it facing the bird inside the nest.

### FURTHERING YOUR SKILLS
This cake is a perfect baby shower cake. Make the birds pink for a girl or blue for a boy.

# Fabric effect clutch bag

Every girl loves a nice clutch bag, and this one won't disappoint. The billowing ruffles really do make this cake look like it's covered in delicate fabric and suited to a red carpet event.

**SKILLS FOR REVIEW**
Rolling out fondant and marzipan: page 54
Covering a cake board: page 56
Covering a cake: page 58

## EQUIPMENT

30 cm (12 in.) square cake board

Balling tool (optional)

2 fine paintbrushes, for gluing and painting

6 cm (2 1/4 in.) diameter circle cutter

Paint palette

128 cm (50 in.) ribbon the same width as the cake board edge

Double-sided tape

## INGREDIENTS

18 cm (7 in.) round Madeira cake (see page 24)

3 quantities fondant in white (see page 28)

2 quantities gum paste in black (see page 36)

Edible glue (see page 41)

Lustre dust in gold

Clear alcohol or dipping solution

Edible pearls, to decorate

### STEP 1
To retain as many servings as possible, keep the carving of this cake to a minimum and use ruffles to build its unique shape. Lay the cake on a work surface and cut a slice off one side, about 2.5 cm (1 in.) in from the edge.

### STEP 2
Then cut a wider slice off the other side of the cake, parallel to the first cut. This will become the bottom of the cake, so ensure you remove enough for a stable base. Discard the off-cuts (or turn them into cake pops instead – see page 26). If you have cut the cake on an angle, you may find it leans. You can lay it back down and adjust this, but if you make too many extra cuts, you will be left with very little cake, so try to keep them to a minimum.

### STEP 3
Roll out one-third of the white fondant and cover the cake board, ensuring the edges are sharp and clean. Then stand the cake on its longer edge and cover it with the

remaining white fondant. Remove the excess fondant and then carefully move the cake onto the board using a spatula or cake lifter.

### STEP 4
Roll out the black gum paste until it is around 2 mm (¹/₈ in.) thick and then cut out several circles at a time with the cutter. If you have a slightly thicker edge than you would like, use a balling tool to rub along the edge of the circle to make it thinner. If you do not have this tool, your fingertip will work just as well.

### STEP 5
Fold each circle in half and then half again so that you have a triangle. Do this gently so the gum paste keeps an open shape. You will need approximately 50–60 circles to cover the cake, but it is important to attach the folded circles to the cake as you make them so they dry in position.

6

8

9

### STEP 6

Attach the triangles to the cake using edible glue, starting at the base of the cake. Paint the edible glue onto the cake rather than onto the triangles because the black will transfer to the brush really easily and can become messy. Lay the face of each triangle against the cake surface with the open edges pointing down and the bottom corners adjoining each other. With each new layer, stagger the triangles so you cover the base fondant colour. This will help with the shape of the cake and give fuller coverage.

### STEP 7

Build up the layers until you have just a 3 cm (1 ¼ in.) gap left at the top of the bag. Take a small piece of the fondant you have used for the ruffles and roll it out until it is around 3 mm (⅛ in.) thick. Cut it into a rectangle measuring 3 x 6 cm (1 ¼ x 2 ½ in.) – you are trying to cover the top of the bag to give it a flat surface. Attach this piece using edible glue.

### STEP 8

To make the bag's clasp, roll out the white fondant until it is 1 cm (½ in.) thick and then cut out a rectangle measuring about 2 x 5 cm (¾ x 2 in.). It needs to be big enough to be seen from all angles of the cake. If you make it too small, it will become hidden by the ruffles.

### STEP 9

Attach the clasp to the cake using edible glue, then, using a sharp knife, make an indentation along the length of the fondant.

### STEP 10

Take two gobstopper-sized pieces from the white fondant off-cuts, roll them into balls, and attach them both to the centre of the strip to represent the clasp.

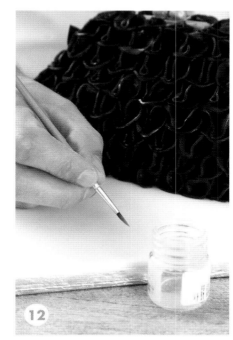

### STEP 11

Mix a pea-sized amount of the gold powder with a few drops of clear alcohol or dipping solution in the paint palette. Apply the paint to the clasp of the bag, covering both the strip and the two balls. Be careful to paint these areas only and not the ruffles. If you find the colour is not intense enough, let the paint dry and put on a second coat.

### STEP 12

Paint an outline of a necklace with edible glue onto the cake board. Keep the line organic and not as a rigid oval, and this will look more lifelike once you have attached the pearls.

### STEP 13

Attach the pearls one-by-one to form a necklace. Fasten the ribbon around the edge of the board with double-sided tape, making sure the join is at the back of the board.

### FURTHERING YOUR SKILLS

- I have covered the board in a different coloured fondant to the bag to make it easier to see the ruffles. Don't feel you have to do the same thing – you could always cover the board to match the ruffles. Either option works well.

- When choosing the colour of the ribbon for the board, I always like to use something to match the cake, so it seems like part of the design.

- If you have used corn flour when rolling out the fondant, take a clean brush dipped in clear alcohol or dipping solution and paint over any corn flour marks. They will instantly vanish and the alcohol will quickly evaporate, leaving you with a perfect finish.

# Snowflake cake

Christmas wouldn't be complete without a lovely cake. This particular one is beautiful, and I am sure your loved ones will enjoy it both to look at and devour.

## SKILLS FOR REVIEW

Covering a cake board: page 56
Filling and crumb coating
a cake: page 50
Covering a cake: page 58
Achieving a good modelling
consistency: page 207
Using the scriber tool: page 159
Using cutters and moulds: page 208

## EQUIPMENT

23 cm (9 in.) diameter round
cake board

80 cm (30 in.) white satin ribbon the
same width as the cake board edge

Double-sided tape

JEM snowflake plastic cupcake cutter

JEM foam board

Scriber tool

Fine paintbrush, for gluing

## INGREDIENTS

1 quantity fondant in red
(see page 34)

18 cm (7 in.) round basic sponge cake
(see page 20)

1 quantity gum paste in white
(see page 36)

1 quantity frosting in your chosen colour
and flavour (see page 28)

Lustre dust in pearl

Edible glue (see page 41)

## FURTHERING YOUR SKILLS

As you become more accomplished at removing the snowflakes from the cutters, you will be able to do it sooner after you have cut them. You may then be able to remove them when they are still soft and attach them to the curved corners of cakes.

### STEP 1
Roll out the red fondant and cover the cake board, ensuring the edges are sharp and clean. Allow the fondant to dry and then fasten the ribbon around the edge of the board with double-sided tape.

### STEP 2
Using the frosting, fill and crumb coat the cake. Then roll out the red fondant and cover the cake.

### STEP 3
To make the snowflakes, first knead the gum paste until it is flexible and easy to work with. Then roll out a piece until it is 1 mm ($1/24$ in.) thick at the most.

### STEP 4
Place the snowflake cutters on the foam board and then place the gum paste over them. Roll a rolling pin over the gum paste so it presses into the cutters. Roll over the paste several times until you can clearly see the snowflakes through the paste. Carefully remove the excess from the outside. You will need about 25–30 snowflakes to cover the cake.

### STEP 5
Let the snowflakes dry for about 15 minutes. Then use the scriber tool to gently remove unwanted sections of the snowflakes. Just insert the pin tip and lift away. To remove the snowflake itself, insert the scriber tool into the paste but not enough to pass all the way through the paste. Then lift up and away from the cutter. You may need to tease sections from the cutter before it will all lift away.

### STEP 6
Place the snowflakes on kitchen roll and dust with the pearl lustre.

### STEP 7
Attach the snowflakes to the cake around the sides and on top using the edible glue.

# Birthday cake

This design is great for those occasions when you want to make a feature of the birthday girl or boy's age on top of the cake.

**SKILLS FOR REVIEW**
Filling and crumb coating
a cake: page 50
Covering a cake: page 58

## EQUIPMENT

5 mm (¼ in.) circle plunger cutter

Lollypop stick

Large number cutter

2 cm (¾ in.) diameter circle cutter

Craft knife

Fine paintbrush, for gluing

## INGREDIENTS

18 cm (7 in.) round basic sponge cake
   (see page 20)

1 quantity frosting in your chosen colour
   and flavour (see page 28)

1 quantity fondant in white
   (see page 34)

1 quantity gum paste, divided into blue,
   yellow and red (see page 36)

Small quantity of royal icing
   (see page 40)

Edible glue (see page 41)

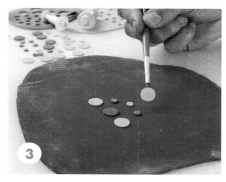

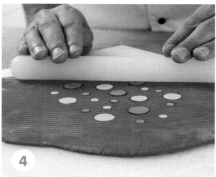

## FURTHERING YOUR SKILLS

- Add an attractive array of stars and spirals to this design for a really fun look.

- You could also add a name to the cake, making each letter exactly as you would for the number featured on this particular design.

### STEP 1

Using the frosting, fill and crumb coat the cake. Then roll out the white fondant and cover the cake.

### STEP 2

Roll out golf ball-sized pieces of blue and yellow paste. Cut small dots from each with the circle plunger cutter.

### STEP 3

Roll out a larger piece of the red paste until it is 5 mm (¼ in.) thick and big enough for the number cutter. Then carefully stick the dots onto the paste using a little edible glue. Position them in a random pattern.

### STEP 4

Once you have glued down all the dots, carefully roll over the red paste with a rolling pin, keeping the pressure even.

### STEP 5

Use the number cutter to cut out the shape and immediately turn it over with the plain side facing upwards.

### STEP 6

Take the lollypop stick and dip 4 cm (1¾ in.) of it into the royal icing. Place it on the back of the number and leave half of the stick protruding from the base of the number. Let this dry until the number holds its own shape.

### STEP 7

Roll out the remaining paste colours to 3 mm (⅛ in.) thick and cut out lots of the 2 cm (¾ in.) circles from each colour. Roll each circle into a ball and stick around the bottom edge of the cake with edible glue. To finish, stick the number into the centre of the cake.

# Jungle cake

I love the little characters on this cake – they make it such a joy to look at. You could add many more to this design as your skills develop.

**SKILLS FOR REVIEW**

Achieving a good modelling consistency: page 207
Filling and crumb coating the cake: page 50
Covering a cake: page 58
Dowelling a cake: page 62
Using the scriber tool: page 159

## EQUIPMENT

Large letter cutters (for the name)

2 fine paintbrushes, for gluing and painting

Paint palette

Lollypop sticks

Scriber tool

Balling tool

Craft knife

Leaf plunger cutter

## INGREDIENTS

2 quantities gum paste in gray, white, black, yellow, red, dark brown, light brown and green

Food colouring paste in black and brown

Clear alcohol or dipping solution

13 cm (5 in.) round basic sponge cake (see page 20)

18 cm (7 in.) round basic sponge cake (see page 20)

2 quantities frosting in your chosen colour and flavour (see page 28)

1 quantity fondant in blue and yellow (see page 34)

Small amount of royal icing (see page 40)

Edible glue (see page 41)

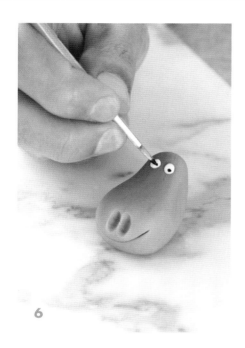

### STEP 1

To make the standing letters for the name, roll out the white gum paste and cut out the name using the letter cutters.

### STEP 2

Mix the black food colouring with the clear alcohol or dipping solution in the paint palette and then paint a zebra print pattern across each letter. Allow the paint to dry, then flip the letters over.

### STEP 3

Take the lollypop sticks and dip about 4 cm (1 ³/₄ in.) of each one into the royal icing. Place one on the back of the each letter, leaving half of the stick protruding from the base of each one. Let this dry until the royal icing is set firm and the letters are able to hold their own shape while you decorate the rest of the cake.

### STEP 4

To make the hippo, roll a ball of gray gum paste on its side to thin out one end slightly. Use your fingers to mould the head shape and sit it onto the work surface so the back becomes flat.

### STEP 5

Use the scriber tool to scribe in a mouth and then insert the small end of the balling tool into the paste above the mouth and gently pull down a little to make the nostrils.

### STEP 6

Roll two tiny balls of white paste for the eyes. Glue them to the face and add a dot of black to each eye for the pupil.

### STEP 7

Take three tiny balls of gray paste and use the balling tool to fix two of them on the top of the head as ears. Use your fingertips to pinch the tips of the ears.

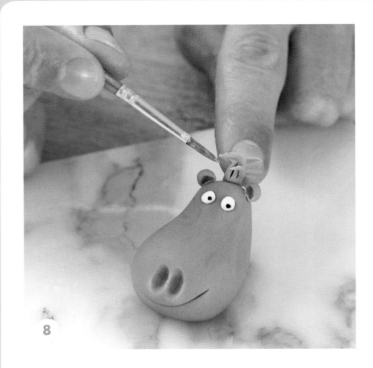

8

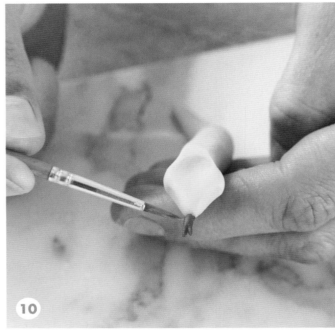

10

## STEP 8

Roll the final ball into a cylinder shape and use the craft knife to make two vertical lines almost the full length of the strip. Tease the pieces apart slightly, then glue it in place as a tuft of hair in the centre of the head.

## STEP 9

To make the snake, roll a piece of yellow paste into a long thin cylinder with one rounded tip and one pointed end 8 cm (3 ¼ in.) long. At the rounded end, flatten the last 3 cm (1 ¼ in.) of the strip so it becomes a circle. Pinch the end slightly, then turn it through 45 degrees toward the pointed tip. This will form the head of the snake.

## STEP 10

Add a tiny red piece of paste and use the craft knife to cut it into two to form a forked tongue. Paint on two tiny dots for the eyes with the black food colouring paste mixed with a drop of clear alcohol or dipping solution,

and lean the snake against something while it dries. Curve the other half of the snake and let it dry for 40 minutes.

## STEP 11

Making the gorilla is my favourite job on this cake. Take a golf ball-sized piece of the black gum paste and roll it into a ball. Sit it on the work surface and gently press down on it with your thumb so the back becomes flat and the top is less rounded. Now roll two small balls of gray gum paste and press them down so they are flat. Glue them on halfway up the face. Then roll a slightly bigger ball of the gray paste and flatten it again. Stick it over the base of those two circles you just attached plus the bottom half of the face. Use your finger to smooth the circles together so the join disappears.

## STEP 12

Take the small end of the balling tool, insert it into the paste, lift a little, then pull the tool down just a small way

12    14    16

into the paste. This will raise the top of the nostril and give depth to the bottom of it. Repeat this for the second nostril.

## STEP 13
Roll two tiny balls of white paste and add them to the face as eyes. Flatten them using your fingertip and then paint on the pupils with the black food colouring paint.

## STEP 14
Use the pointed end of the scriber tool to scribe in a smile. Then use the rounded end to gently press the bottom lip down on one section. This will open the gorilla's mouth slightly and make him more animated.

## STEP 15
Finally, roll two tiny balls and use the balling tool to pick them up and attach them as ears on the sides of the gorilla's head. To give the gorilla fur, use the pointed tip of

the scriber tool to flick the surface of the head in various directions. Do this just on the black parts and leave the gray skin areas smooth.

## STEP 16
For the lion's head, take a ball of the dark brown paste and flatten it to become a thick circle. Now use the scriber tool to make outward indentations for the mane. Do this all around the circle for several minutes.

## STEP 17
Use a small ball of the light brown paste to make the lion's face. Stick it onto the centre of the mane, then flatten it with your thumb. Roll two small balls of the light paste and flatten them, then stick them on the bottom of the face side by side as cheeks.

18

19

### STEP 18

To make the nose, roll a tiny ball of the dark brown paste and stick them between the cheeks at the top. For the eyes, roll two small balls of white paste and add them to the face just above the cheeks and nose. Smooth them down using your finger and then paint on the pupils.

### STEP 19

To create the giraffe print, dilute brown food colouring paste with clear alcohol or dipping solution and dab onto the cake with a piece of sponge. Aim for a slightly rounded edge to the shapes rather than straight lines, and none of the shapes should be the same.

### STEP 20

While the characters' heads dry, use the frosting to fill and crumb coat each of the cakes, but don't stack them yet. Roll out the blue fondant and cover the larger cake,

then repeat with the yellow fondant and cover the smaller cake. Dowel the cakes together, with the smaller cake on top.

### STEP 21

Dab the patches onto the top cake, leaving a gap between each one so you can see the yellow background showing through. Continue adding the patches to the cake until the whole top tier is covered.

### STEP 22

For the bottom tier, you want to make this look like a jungle. To start, roll out the green paste and use the craft knife to cut out about 3 long, thin leaf shapes. Attach these leaves at the front of the bottom tier using a small dab of the edible glue. Then stick the lion's head on the top of them and allow it to set.

22

24

### STEP 23
Roll out more of the green paste and cut out about 10 leaves with the plunger cutter. Stick the hippo head and gorilla about 2.5 cm (1 in.) on either side of the lion's head. Then build up the leaves between and under each of the heads.

### STEP 24
Stick the snake on the bottom tier, so that he looks out from the cake.

### STEP 25
Roll the remaining gray paste and mould it into rocks. Stick them in position around the base of the cake in clusters with more leaves behind them.

### STEP 26
To finish the cake, carefully place the name into the top tier, then stand back and admire your handiwork.

---

**FURTHERING YOUR SKILLS**

- Make the characters ahead of time and you will find this cake is easily made in an afternoon.

- If you are having a small party, simply make a single tier cake and decorate it as a jungle.

# Two-tier wedding cake

Now that you have learned so many frosting skills, this wedding cake is readily achievable. It would be perfect for a smaller wedding as it still has the impact of a multi-tiered cake (see page 282) and is every bit as beautiful.

**SKILLS FOR REVIEW**
Covering a cake board: page 56
Filling and crumb coating
a cake: page 50
Making a ruffle: page 214
Making a corsage: page 212

## EQUIPMENT

23 cm (9 in.) diameter round
cake board

80 cm (30 in.) pale blue ribbon the
same width as the cake board edge

Double-sided tape

2 fine paintbrushes, for gluing
and painting

Scriber tool

## INGREDIENTS

13 cm (5 in.) round basic sponge cake
(see page 20)

18 cm (7 in.) round basic sponge cake
(see page 20)

3 quantities fondant in ivory
(see page 34)

2 quantities frosting in your chosen
colour and flavour (see page 28)

1 quantity gum paste in pale blue and
ivory (see page 36)

Edible glue (see page 41)

Lustre dust in pearl

## FURTHERING YOUR SKILLS

**Add some edible pearls around the central circle of the corsages. This will make the wedding cake look even more luxurious.**

### STEP 1

Roll out a third of the ivory fondant and cover the cake board, ensuring the edges are sharp and clean. Allow the fondant to dry and then fasten the ribbon around the edge of the board with double-sided tape.

### STEP 2

Using the frosting, fill and crumb coat each of the cakes, but don't stack them yet.

### STEP 3

Roll out the remaining ivory fondant and cover both cakes individually. Set aside to dry, then dowel the cakes together, ready to be decorated.

### STEP 4

Using the ivory gum paste, make a ruffle and stick it to the cake so that it runs vertically up the cake. Paint a thick line of glue in a vertical line up the centre of the ruffle on the bottom tier and across the top until it meets the top cake. Carefully glue the centre strip in place starting at the base of the top cake and working down to the bottom.

### STEP 5

Using the pale blue gum paste for the outside set of petals for each flower, and the ivory paste for the smaller set of petals, make a corsage and attach the three elements to the cake in a cluster. Use more of the pale blue gum paste for the small balls in the centre of the flower. Set aside and allow everything to set.

### STEP 6

To finish, use a little pearl lustre and a dry brush to highlight the ruffle and corsage.

# Working with marzipan

Many people enjoy working with marzipan and in some countries they use only marzipan for cake decoration. It's a different consistency to fondant, although you can do most of the things that are possible with fondant and in this chapter I show you how.

# Texturising marzipan

Sometimes when modelling with marzipan you need more than a flat finish and texturising is required.

### STEP 1
Make sure the marzipan is pliable and soft before you begin to add texture. Knead it until it is soft and warm as it will take on the texture much better than if it is cold.

### STEP 2
Depending on the texture effect you are looking to achieve, you will need to source the right tool. Experimentation is the key here. For example, if you have made marzipan fruits such as oranges and lemons and you want to achieve a peel texture, you will find that rolling the shaped marzipan over a fruit zester achieves the perfect finish.

**USING THIS SKILL**
Marzipan Fruits: page 254

---

### EQUIPMENT

*Texturiser of your choice*

---

### FURTHERING YOUR SKILLS

When searching for an appropriate tool to texturise your marzipan, remember that the amount of pressure applied can also affect the final result.

# Glazing marzipan

With certain models and decorations it is important to have a reflective glazed surface.

### STEP 1

If you use edible glaze from a small pot, it is important to know that it has a very thin consistency and spreads very easily. As with most things in cake decoration, less is more, and it is better to build up your glaze than to have it seeping onto other decorations by accident.

### STEP 2

If you use an aerosol glaze, you will need to make your own spraying booth inside a cardboard box. This is because the glaze spreads incredibly far when sprayed and can alter a design if it falls in the wrong place.

### STEP 3

A single layer of glaze will give a basic shine to the surface of the marzipan. For a high gloss finish, you will need to apply several coats. This applies to both the small pots of glaze and the aerosol. Let dry, and then use to decorate cakes and cupcakes.

**USING THIS SKILL**
Marzipan Fruits: page 254

## EQUIPMENT

*Edible glaze*

*Fine paintbrush (optional)*

### FURTHERING YOUR SKILLS

**To remove the glaze from paintbrushes, use a little clear alcohol or dipping solution. It is incredibly hard to remove so it is best to use a paintbrush that you don't mind disposing of afterwards if necessary.**

# Marzipan fruits

From autumn fruit basket cakes to individual cupcakes, these fruits will adorn them perfectly. For small items like this, there is no need to add CMC powder to the marzipan – just go ahead and use it straight from the package.

**SKILLS FOR REVIEW**
Texturising marzipan: page 252
Glazing marzipan: page 253

## EQUIPMENT

Cone tool

Star plunger cutter

Star tool

Cheese grater with zesting side

Fine paintbrush

## INGREDIENTS

Marzipan in a light natural colour and in red, green, light green and orange (see page 37)

Dried cloves

Dust colours in red, green and light brown

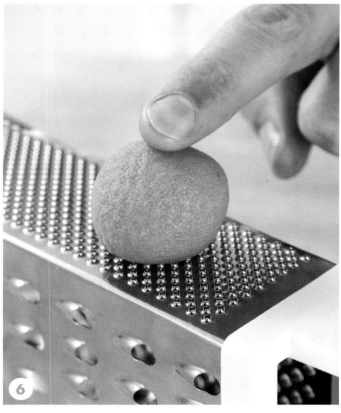

### STEP 1

To make the strawberry, take a small ball of the red marzipan and roll it on one side until it looks like a strawberry.

### STEP 2

Use the small end of the cone tool to make the texture of a strawberry by pricking the surface all over.

### STEP 3

Roll out a small piece of the green marzipan, and cut a small star using the plunger cutter. Add it to the top of the strawberry and then use the star tool to press into the centre of the green star.

### STEP 4

For the apple, take a small piece of the light green marzipan and roll it into a ball. Use the large end of the cone tool to press into the centre of the ball to create the top of the apple.

### STEP 5

Take a clove and break away the stalk from the flower part. Place this in the centre of the apple where you have just made the indentation. Press the flower part into the base of the apple.

### STEP 6

To make the orange, take a piece of the orange marzipan and roll it into a perfect ball shape. Roll it over the zesting side of the cheese grater to give it a realistic orange peel texture.

### STEP 7

Roll out a small amount of the green paste and cut a tiny star using the plunger cutter. Place the star in the centre of the orange and use the star tool to press it into the orange.

### STEP 8

Finally, to make the pear, take the natural uncoloured marzipan and roll a small piece into a ball. Then gently use your fingertips to mould it into a pear shape. Take a clove, and as with the apple, split the clove and add the stalk to the top of the pear at an angle and the flower to the base of the pear.

### STEP 9

Set all the pieces of fruit aside for around 30 minutes to dry before decorating them.

### STEP 10

To finish the decoration, use the dusting powders to add colour. The technique is exactly the same as for shading on fondant. For the apple, take a small amount of the red dusting powder and lightly build up colour on one side of the fruit. For the pear, build up the green dusting colour across the fruit in varying tones and then dust one side of the pear with the brown powder.

---

#### FURTHERING YOUR SKILLS

- **To give your fruits a glossy finish, coat them with a spray glaze.**

- **When making apples and pears, you can add a small dusting of cinnamon to the marzipan to give a speckled surface pattern to the fruits.**

---

# Teddy bear cake topper

Like many of the other designs in this chapter, this little chap works equally well made in either modelling marzipan or gum paste. He can be adapted for so many occasions that you will soon find you have a little army of teddy bears to add to every cake.

## EQUIPMENT

Craft knife

Scriber tool

2 fine paintbrushes, for gluing
    and painting

Stitching tool

Paint palette

## INGREDIENTS

1 quantity modelling marzipan in dark brown, light brown and black
    (see page 37)

Edible glue (see page 41)

Food colouring powder in black and white

Clear alcohol or dipping solution

## STEP 1

Roll a large ball of the dark brown marzipan for the body. Form a wide cylinder shape and then sit it on your work surface and gently mould the top half until it is slightly thinner.

## STEP 2

Roll out two thin cylinders of the dark brown marzipan and use the craft knife to cut them both in half diagonally. Set two of the pieces to one side and take the other two to make the legs. Use the stitching tool to run a line down the centre of the body.

## STEP 3

The trimmed ends will become the surface that attaches to the teddy bear's body. Gently turn the other end of each leg to make the feet and flatten the bottom with your finger to create a flat paw.

## STEP 4

Use the scriber tool to indent two lines on the top of each foot. Then indent with a small round cutter and piping tip. Using the edible glue, stick the legs to the bear.

### STEP 5

Take the other two lengths of marzipan and gently smooth them onto the work surface until slightly flattened. Add two lines at the rounded ends of the paws and then stick the arms to the body.

### STEP 6

For the teddy bear's head, roll a small ball of the light brown marzipan and gently flatten it on the front to form his face. Run the stitching tool over the centre of the head.

### STEP 7

To make the ears, roll two tiny balls of dark brown marzipan and then use the balling tool to pick them up one by one and stick them to the top of the head on each side.

### STEP 8

To make the teddy's snout, take a small piece of the light brown marzipan and roll it into a pea-sized ball. Flatten it with your finger and glue it in the centre of the face. Use the scriber tool to scribe a line down the middle of the snout and then roll a tiny ball of the pale brown marzipan and attach it as his nose.

### STEP 9

Use a tiny amount of the black marzipan to roll two small balls for the eyes. Stick them to the face close together

and in the centre above the snout. Flatten them slightly with a fingertip.

## STEP 10

Mix a small amount of the white food colouring with the clear alcohol or dipping solution in the paint palette and paint a tiny dot to the top right of each eye. This will give your teddy bear a lifelike appearance as it will look like light reflecting off the bear.

## STEP 11

For the final touch of characterisation, mix a small amount of the black powder with the alcohol as for the white colouring and add two fine eyebrows to the bear.

### FURTHERING YOUR SKILLS

**To make a feminine bear, change the colouring to pink or yellow and add a dusting of pink to each side of her snout.**

# Cheese slice cake

This fun design is great for everyone young and old to enjoy. These cute mice will become a party favourite with their cheeky smiles and cute tails.

## SKILLS FOR REVIEW
Covering a cake board: page 56
Filling and crumb coating
a cake: page 50
Covering a cake: page 58

## EQUIPMENT

23 cm (9 in.) diameter round
    cake board

Melon baller

2 cm (³/₄ in.) diameter circle cutter

Craft knife

Fine paintbrush, for gluing

Scriber tool

## INGREDIENTS

18 cm (7 in.) square Madeira cake
    (see page 24)

1 quantity fondant in pale blue
    (see page 34)

1 quantity frosting in your chosen colour
    and flavour (see page 28)

750 g (1 lb. 2 oz.) uncoloured marzipan

1 quantity modelling marzipan in gray,
    white and pink (see page 37)

Edible glue (see page 41)

Edible food pen in black

### STEP 1

Using the fondant, cover the cake board, ensuring the edges are sharp and clean.

### STEP 2

Take the cake and slice it diagonally, then turn the two pieces so they sit in the same direction. Carefully fill the cake with frosting and place the cake on its side on a surface with the longest side facing upwards.

### STEP 3

Use the melon baller to cut out 5–6 holes across the surface of the cake. Simply insert and twist to keep the holes the same size as the melon baller. Leave an area untouched by holes on both the top and side of the cake.

### STEP 4

Now you need two larger holes for the mice to use. These will go in the two areas you have kept blank. Use the baller to make the holes, but this time gently cut away more of the cake for a larger hole.

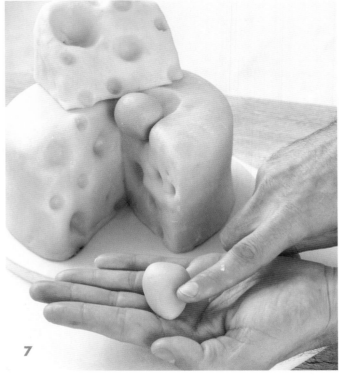

### STEP 5

With more of the frosting, crumb coat the cake and use the back of a spoon to smooth the frosting into the holes.

### STEP 6

Roll out the uncoloured marzipan and use it to cover the cake. Smooth it down across the top and gently into each of the holes. Cut away the excess marzipan and leave a neat edge to the cake. Then transfer to the cake board and stack the smaller slice on the bigger cake.

### STEP 7

Roll two small balls from the gray marzipan, then stick one in one of the holes with edible glue. Roll the other ball on its side to create a point to one side. This will become the nose of a mouse.

### STEP 8

To make the first mouse's ears, roll out a small amount of the gray marzipan and cut out two small circles using the 2 cm (³/₄ in.) circle cutter. Use the craft knife to cut a small piece away from the bottom of each circle to give them a straight edge, then pinch the marzipan together at the straight edge. Attach each of the ears to the cone-shaped piece of gray marzipan.

### STEP 9

For the eyes, take a tiny ball of the white marzipan, divide it into two small balls, and flatten each with your fingertip. Glue them to the face of the mouse, just below the ears. To finish the eyes, add a pupil to each eye using the edible food pen.

8

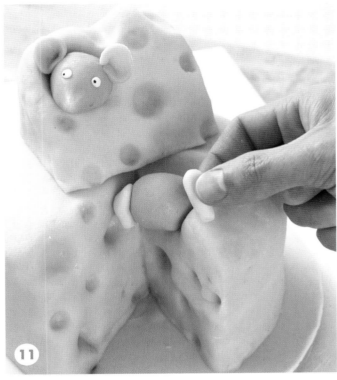

11

### STEP 10

Stick the mouse head into the other hole so that she is facing outwards.

### STEP 11

To finish the other mouse, roll two pea-sized balls of the pink marzipan and model them into cylinder shapes. Use the craft knife to cut two lines at one end of each cylinder to delineate the toes. Roll each toe gently in your fingertips to round them and make them longer. Attach both feet to the mouse's body that is already sitting in the other hole. Leave a small gap between the heels.

### STEP 12

Take another small gobstopper-sized piece of pink marzipan and roll it into a long tail. Use the scriber tool to make small indentations along the tail and then stick it to the bottom of the mouse.

---

#### FURTHERING YOUR SKILLS

**Use icing sugar to dust your work surface when working with marzipan. If you use corn flour, it can react with the marzipan.**

# Animal cupcakes

## Chick cupcakes

These super cute chicks would be ideal for celebrating a baby shower or maybe a farm-themed birthday party. These would also look great at any Easter table.

**SKILLS FOR REVIEW**
Flat topping a cupcake: page 66

### EQUIPMENT

Palette knife

8 cm (3 ¼ in.) diameter circle cutter

Scriber tool

Fine paintbrush, for gluing

### INGREDIENTS

12 cupcakes from the basic recipe (see page 23)

1 quantity frosting in your chosen colour and flavour (see page 28)

500 g (1 lb. 2 oz.) marzipan in yellow, orange and black (see page 37)

Edible glue (see page 41)

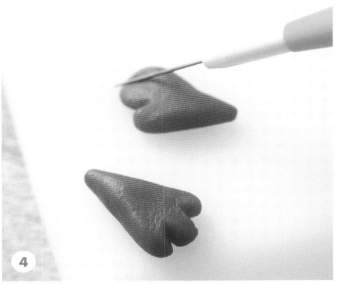

### STEP 1
Using the palette knife, flat top each cupcake, finishing with a circle of the yellow marzipan

### STEP 2
Roll three balls of the orange marzipan. Two must be gobstopper-sized and the third one the size of a large pea.

### STEP 3
To make the chick's webbed feet, take the two larger balls and flatten them using your fingertips to make them into a teardrop shape. Then pinch the base of each teardrop into a point.

### STEP 4
Use the scriber tool make two incisions in the rounded end of the shapes, then use the same tool to separate the toes. Roll them gently between your finger and thumb to smooth out each toe. Attach the feet to the chick using edible glue.

### STEP 5
Roll the third orange ball into a cone by gently rolling on one side of the ball. Work with the marzipan until you are happy with the beak shape and then stand it on a surface to create a flat bottom to the beak. Attach the beak to the face using edible glue.

### STEP 6
Finally, take a very small piece of the black marzipan, split it into two pieces and roll into balls for the chick's eyes. These need to be small enough to fit the design and should you go too big, you will find the bird looks a little stunned. Attach the eyes using edible glue.

### FURTHERING YOUR SKILLS
You could vary the design of this cute little chick by using a sharp knife to cut the beak horizontally and give the little fellow an open mouth.

# Frog cupcakes

These little frogs are great fun to make and hugely successful at any children's party.

**SKILLS FOR REVIEW**
Using cutters and moulds: page 208

## EQUIPMENT

Palette knife

10 cm (4 in.) diameter circle cutter

2 fine paintbrushes, for gluing
  and painting

## INGREDIENTS

12 cupcakes from the basic recipe
  (see page 23)

1 quantity frosting in your chosen colour
  and flavour (see page 28)

500 g (1 lb. 2 oz.) marzipan in green
  (see page 37)

White edible balls the size of a large
  pearl or small pea

Edible glue (see page 41)

Food colouring powder in black

## STEP 1
Using a palette knife, build up a rounded dome of frosting on top of each cupcake.

## STEP 2
Roll out the green marzipan until it is about 3 mm (⅛ in.) thick. Cut out a circle using the cutter, place the circle over the top of the cupcake, and gently smooth down the edges.

## STEP 3
For the eyes, stick two of the white balls near the top of the cupcake. Once they have dried, paint a pupil on each eye using the black food colouring. Put a small circle of green marzipan behind each eye for eyelids.

You would usually mix the food colouring with clear alcohol or dipping solution to form a paint, but here the white edible balls have a shiny surface and so the colouring will adhere better if painted on neat. Make an indentation for the mouth with a circle cutter, paint on the mouth and add two dots for the nose. Finish with a red cylinder, curled as a tongue.

### FURTHERING YOUR SKILLS

For a more feminine-looking frog, cut a small bow out of modelling marzipan in whatever colour takes your fancy and attach it just to one side at the top of the face.

# Pig cupcakes

This little pig will have all of your guests smiling. Teamed with some of my other designs, such as the Chick and Cow Cupcakes (see pages 266 and 180) you could have a whole farm selection, ideal for any child's birthday party.

**SKILLS FOR REVIEW**
Flat topping a cupcake: page 66

## EQUIPMENT

Palette knife

8 cm (3 ¼ in.) diameter round cutter

Craft knife

Balling tool

2 fine paintbrushes, for gluing and painting

Scriber tool

Paint palette

## INGREDIENTS

12 cupcakes from the basic recipe (see page 23)

1 quantity frosting in your chosen colour and flavour (see page 28)

1 quantity modelling marzipan in pink (see page 37)

Edible glue (see page 41)

Food colouring paste in black

Clear alcohol or dipping solution

### STEP 1

Using the palette knife, flat top each cupcake, building up the surface more than usual for a slightly domed top and finishing with a circle of the pink marzipan.

### STEP 2

Roll a small piece of the marzipan out until it is very thin, then use the craft knife to cut out two triangles. Stick them to the face at the top on either side with the edible glue and finish them by folding over the top of each triangle.

### STEP 3

To make the nose, roll out another small piece of the marzipan to about 5 mm (¼ in.) thick and use the craft knife to cut a small oval. Stick the nose to the face and use the balling tool to create two nostrils in the nose.

### STEP 4

Use the scriber tool to scribe a mouth under the nose and then use the smaller end of the balling tool to give the pig dimples at each end of the smile.

### STEP 5

Finish your happy pig by painting two tiny eyes just above the nose using the black food colouring mixed with a drop of the clear alcohol or dipping solution in the paint palette.

---

#### FURTHERING YOUR SKILLS

**Make different expressions on your pigs to give them more character – a big smile, a frown or even a small curl on his head.**

---

# Working with royal icing

Royal icing is often used when making elegant wedding cakes. It is rigid when dry and is ideal when decorating with piping as it will hold its shape. Royal icing can also be coloured as you please. Either keep it white, colour it with food colourings or use a paint made from lustre dust and alcohol. It also makes great glue as it sets so firm.

# Making brush embroidery

Brush embroidery looks just like the royal icing has been sewn into the cake's surface. It is a delicate finish and incredibly popular.

**USING THIS SKILL**
Brush Embroidery Cupcakes:
page 278

## EQUIPMENT

*Wilton No. 2 round decorating tip*

*Piping bag*

*Square-ended paintbrush*

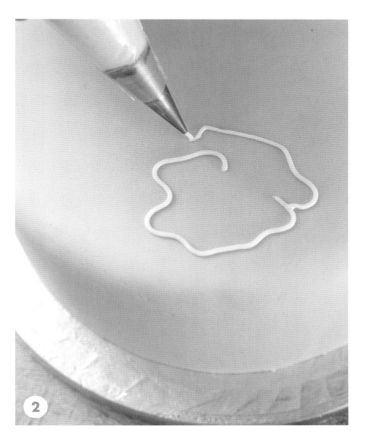

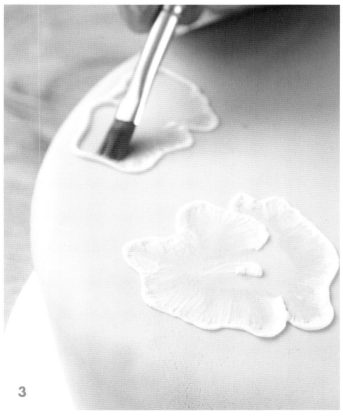

### STEP 1
Secure the tip in your piping bag and then fill it with royal icing.

### STEP 2
Pipe the outer edges of the flower in either a single or double semicircle shape.

### STEP 3
Use a lightly dampened paintbrush to sweep the icing inwards, creating the stitch effect.

# Making cornelli lace

Cornelli lace is a beautiful addition to any cake and incredibly popular for weddings.

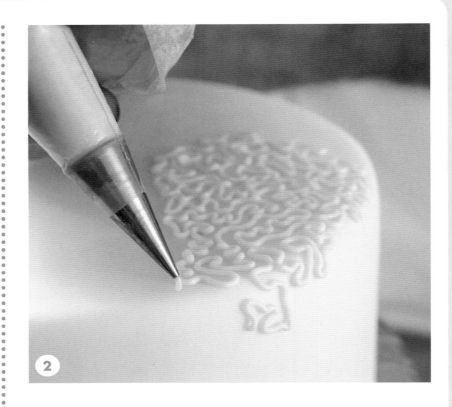

**USING THIS SKILL**
Cornelli Lace Wedding Cake:
page 280

## FURTHERING YOUR SKILLS

You can easily change the effect of cornelli lace icing by choosing to pipe in the same or different colour to the fondant base. Piping in white on a white fondant base is far more subtle than, say, white on a coloured fondant.

### STEP 1
Secure the tip in your piping bag and then fill it with royal icing.

### STEP 2
Pipe a continuous single line of icing in a random manner to cover the whole surface of the cake. The line should meander its way over the surface, but never touch itself. If you have to stop piping at any time to adjust your bag, just stop and then continue from the same place when you restart. The royal icing will settle and hide any joins.

## EQUIPMENT

*Wilton No. 2 round decorating tip*          *Piping bag*

# Piping pearls and dots

Sometimes when you are decorating a cake you need a little extra decoration that you can't achieve with fondant or modelling paste, such as these pearls and dots. This is when royal icing is the solution. For general piping tips, see piping techniques on page 74.

## USING THIS SKILL
**Three-tier Wedding Cake: page 282**

## STEP 1
Piping pearls and dots to embellish other decorations on a cake is a popular choice and simple to do. Secure the tip in your piping bag and then fill it with royal icing and pipe the pearls and dots to the size you require.

## STEP 2
Use a damp paintbrush to remove any tails from your piping. Once dry, you can dust these pearls with a lustre dust or paint for added interest.

## FURTHERING YOUR SKILLS
Pipe the pearls in white and then colour them using food colouring powder mixed with clear alcohol or dipping solution. If you make a mistake, it's easier to remove the white pearl than if you have used coloured royal icing.

## EQUIPMENT

Piping bag

Wilton No. 3 round decorating tip

Fine paintbrush

# Brush embroidery cupcakes

Once you have mastered the art of brush embroidery, you will find yourself using this pleasing skill to decorate cupcakes and other cakes galore.

**SKILLS FOR REVIEW**
Flat topping a cupcake: page 66
Making brush embroidery:
page 274

## EQUIPMENT

*Palette knife*

*Piping bag*

*Wilton No. 2 round decorating tip*

*Square-ended paintbrush*

## INGREDIENTS

*12 cupcakes from the basic recipe (see page 23)*

*1 quantity frosting in your chosen colour and flavour (see page 28)*

*1 quantity fondant in your chosen colour (see page 34)*

*1 quantity royal icing (see page 40), made slightly looser in consistency*

## STEP 1

Flat top each cupcake using frosting and fondant in your chosen colour.

## STEP 2

Secure the tip in your piping bag and then fill it with the royal icing. Start by piping a three-petalled flower and then pull a damp paintbrush through the piped icing in toward the centre of the cake. Don't break the outer line of piping with the brush, but drag the icing in from the inner edge of the piped line. Always use inward strokes and turn the cupcake if it makes it easier to reach the area you are working on.

## STEP 3

Pipe another two petals over the first layer and repeat the brush strokes. Then pipe a second layer of petals within the first to add fullness.

## STEP 4

Once you get to the centre of the flower, pipe a single dot then five more surrounding the first.

### FURTHERING YOUR SKILLS

- **You want your brush to be only slightly damp not wet. This will ensure you are not watering down the royal icing.**

# Cornelli lace wedding cake

This cake is beautiful and will be the perfect centrepiece of any wedding.

### SKILLS FOR REVIEW
Covering a cake board: page 56
Filling and crumb coating a cake: page 50
Covering a cake: page 58
Dowelling a cake: page 62
Making cornelli lace: page 276
Using cutters and moulds: page 208

## EQUIPMENT

23 cm (9 in.) diameter round cake board

80 cm (30 in.) pale blue ribbon the same width as the cake board edge

Double-sided tape

2 fine paintbrushes, for gluing and painting

Brooch mould

Wilton No. 1 round decorating tip

Piping bag

Craft knife

Ruler

Paint palette

## INGREDIENTS

13 cm (5 in.) round basic sponge cake (see page 20)

18 cm (7 in.) round basic sponge cake (see page 20)

2 quantities frosting in your chosen colour and flavour (see page 28)

3 quantities fondant in white and blue (see page 34)

2 quantities royal icing (see page 40), made slightly looser in consistency

Edible glue (see page 41)

Gum paste in white (see page 36)

Lustre dust in gold

Clear alcohol or dipping solution

**FURTHERING YOUR SKILLS**
Practise your piping on a piece of baking parchment before you move on to the cake itself.

## STEP 1
Roll out one-third of the white fondant and cover the cake board, ensuring the edges are sharp and clean. Allow the fondant to dry and then fasten the ribbon around the edge of the board with double-sided tape.

## STEP 2
Using the frosting, fill and crumb coat each of the cakes, but don't stack them yet.

## STEP 3
Roll out the remaining white fondant, half at a time, and cover both cakes individually. Set aside to dry, then dowel the cakes together, ready to be decorated.

## STEP 4
Measure and cut a strip of blue fondant that is 5 cm (2 in.) wide and long enough to go around the top tier. Secure the band around the base of the top tier using edible glue. Keep the join at the back of the cake so it looks perfect.

## STEP 5
Fill the brooch mould with the white gum paste (see page 208) and put it in the freezer for about 15 minutes.

## STEP 6
Meanwhile, secure the tip in your piping bag and then fill it with the royal icing and pipe on the cornelli lace until you have covered all of the bottom tier.

## STEP 7
Remove the brooch mould from the freezer and gently release the brooch from the mould. Let the brooch dry for a further 30 minutes.

## STEP 8
Mix the gold lustre dust with the clear alcohol or dipping solution in the paint palette and use it to paint highlights all around the outer edge of the brooch. Let the paint dry, then attach it in the centre of the blue band on the top tier.

# Three-tier wedding cake

Getting married is one of the most important days of someone's life. It calls for a special cake and this cake is just that. The elegant lace and satin combination, coupled with the delicate daisies means this cake is perfect for any bride and groom to celebrate with.

### SKILLS FOR REVIEW
Covering a cake board: page 56
Filling and crumb coating a cake: page 50
Covering a cake: page 58
Dowelling a cake: page 62
Piping pearls and dots: page 277

## EQUIPMENT

30 cm (12 in.) diameter round cake board

102 cm (40 in.) white satin ribbon the same width as the cake board edge

Double-sided tape

2 m (78 in.) satin ribbon

2 m (78 in.) lace ribbon

Daisy plunger cutter set

Wilton No. 1 round decorating tip

Piping bag

2 fine paintbrushes, for gluing and painting

Paint palette

## INGREDIENTS

13 cm (5 in.) round basic sponge cake (see page 20)

18 cm (7 in.) round basic sponge cake (see page 20)

23 cm (9 in.) round basic sponge cake (see page 20)

3 quantities frosting in your chosen colour and flavour (see page 28)

3 quantities fondant in white (see page 34)

½ quantity royal icing (see page 40)

Lustre dust in pearl

Clear alcohol or dipping solution

### STEP 1

Roll out one-third of the white fondant and cover the cake board, ensuring the edges are sharp and clean. Allow the fondant to dry and then fasten the ribbon around the edge of the board with double-sided tape.

### STEP 2

Using the frosting, fill and crumb coat each of the cakes, but don't stack them yet.

### STEP 3

Roll out the remaining white fondant, half at a time, and cover both cakes individually. Set aside to dry, then dowel the cakes together, ready to be decorated.

### STEP 4

Cut the satin ribbon and lace into three lengths, one to go around each tier with an overlap of 3 cm (1 1/4 in.). Fix the ribbons to each tier using small dots of royal icing to hold it in place with the overlap at the back of the cake. Layer the lace over the satin ribbon so that the bottom edges are level.

### STEP 5

Roll out the white fondant to a thickness of 3 mm (1/8 in.) and cut out about 45 daisies in a variety of sizes as this will add depth to the design. Stick the daisies in place in clusters of three on the cake using a small dot of royal icing. Then leave them to set for 30 minutes before icing.

### STEP 6

Secure the tip in your piping bag and then fill it with the royal icing. Pipe small dots around each petal of one daisy to create a halo of dots. Repeat around each daisy.

### STEP 7

Pipe a pearl (see page 277) in the centre of each daisy to finish each flower. Use a damp paintbrush to round off each of the dots and remove the peaks from the pearls. Set aside to allow the royal icing to dry.

### STEP 8

To finish decorating the cake, mix ½ teaspoon of the lustre dust with a few drops of the clear alcohol or dipping in the paint palette and then carefully paint the pearls and dots to give it a luxury appearance.

---

#### FURTHERING YOUR SKILLS

This cake can be made with as many tiers as you need, just ensure you dowel the cakes well and allow them to dry before you stack them to avoid damaging the fondant.

---

# Index